CHRISTIANITY IN CONFLICT

*Pastoral Renewal books are published by Servant Books in cooperation with The Center for Pastoral Renewal.*

# Christianity in Conflict

## *The Struggle for Christian Integrity and Freedom in Secular Culture*

Edited by
Peter Williamson and Kevin Perrotta

 *A Pastoral Renewal Book*

SERVANT BOOKS
Ann Arbor, Michigan

Copyright © 1986 by The Center for Pastoral Renewal

Book design by Kathleen Schuetz
All rights reserved.
Published by Servant Books
P.O. Box 8617
Ann Arbor, Michigan 48107

86 87 88 89 90   10 9 8 7 6 5 4 3 2 1

Printed in the United States of America

ISBN 0-89283-292-4

# Contents

# Contributors

**William Bentley Ball,** an attorney, is a partner in Ball and Skelly of Harrisburg, Pennsylvania. He has been the lead counsel in 19 cases before the United States Supreme Court dealing with religious liberties. He is the chairman of the Federal Bar Association's committee on constitutional law. Mr. Ball is the author of numerous articles, including "Population Control: Civil and Constitutional Concerns" and "Religion in the Public Schools—The Post-Schempp Years," and was a contributor to a volume entitled *Freedom and Education: The Pierce Case Reconsidered.*

**Deborah Malacky Belonick** is a member of the external affairs department of the Orthodox Church in America. She is a representative of that church to the Faith and Order Commission of the National Council of Churches and is an editor of one of its publications, *Jacob's Well.* She is the author of *Feminism in Christianity: An Orthodox Christian Response,* and she was a contributor to the book, *Women and the Priesthood.*

**Donald Bloesch** is a professor of theology at the University of Dubuque Theological Seminary and an ordained minister in the United Church of Christ. He is past president of the American Theological Society. He has written several books, including *Essentials of Evangelical Theology, The Invaded Church,* and *The Future of Evangelical Christianity.*

**Harold O.J. Brown** is pastor of the Evangelical Reformed Church in Klosters, Switzerland. He is a former professor of biblical and systematic theology at Trinity Evangelical Divinity School, Deerfield, Illinois, and a former associate editor of *Christianity Today*. Dr. Brown is the author of several books, including *Heresies: The Image of Christ in the Mirror of Heresy and Orthodoxy from the Apostles to the Present, Christianity and the Class Struggle,* and *The Reconstruction of the Republic.*

**Stephen B. Clark** is president of the assembly of The Sword of the Spirit, an international ecumenical Christian community. He is the author of several books, including *Man and Woman in Christ, Building Christian Communities,* and *Unordained Elders and Renewal Communities.*

**Charles Colson** is the president of Prison Fellowship International. He is the author of several books, including *Born Again, Life Sentence,* and *Who Speaks for God?*

**James Hitchcock** is a professor of history at St. Louis University. He is the founder and past president of the Fellowship of Catholic Scholars. He is the editor and chairman of the board of *Communio,* an international Catholic review, in the United States. Professor Hitchcock has written several books, including *The Decline and Fall of Radical Catholicism, Catholicism and Modernity,* and *What Is Secular Humanism?*

**Ken Wilson** is the pastor of Emmaus Fellowship, in Ann Arbor, Michigan, and a coordinator of The Word of God, the Ann Arbor branch of an international ecumenical Christian community called The Sword of the Spirit. Mr. Wilson is the author of several books, including *God First, Decision to Love,* and *How to Repair the Wrong You've Done.*

**Bruce Yocum** is executive coordinator of The Sword of the Spirit, an international ecumenical Christian community, and a coordinator of The Word of God, its branch in Ann Arbor, Michigan. He is the director of European Outreach Trust, an evangelistic and community-building organization. He has written *Prophecy: Exercising the Prophetic Gifts of the Spirit in the Church Today*.

# A Nation at War

D URING WORLD WAR II, air forces employed a particularly destructive one-two method of bombardment. A first wave of planes would lay a carpet of explosives, blasting buildings, gas and water mains, electrical lines, and so on. A second wave of planes would then drop incendiary bombs, setting fire to the wreckage. The panic, disorder, broken communications, and low water pressure caused by the first bombing made it difficult for emergency crews to deal with the fires ignited by the second.

Modern society bears some resemblance to this pattern. Technology radically changes people's lives. The factory, the automobile, the television, the jet plane, the computer—these have brought great advantages but have also disrupted relationships in the family, among kin, in the local church body, and elsewhere. Into this society of less-rooted individuals and fragmented relationships, secular values are broadcast: careerism in the university and business worlds, consumerism in advertising, selfism in psychology, individualism in the feminist movement. These incendiary values, conveyed through the mass media and other channels, burn through the created connections between sex and marriage, men and women, mothers and their unborn children, the use of the good things of this world and the priorities of the kingdom that is coming.

It is this broad conflict that has brought together the

contributors to this book. They are Protestants, Catholics, and Orthodox who want to help one another understand the conflict and respond to it.

The basic historic principles of Christian faith and morality face stiff challenges in America and elsewhere in the West today. The challenges occur both within the life of the churches—in theology, biblical studies, clergy training, pastoral care, religious education, evangelism, outreach, family life—and in the realms of secular education, media, business, and government. The authors of this book represent a growing number of Christians who recognize that all Christians face these problems in one way or another in America in the 1980s. While old disagreements among Christian traditions remain unresolved, all Christians face profound common challenges to the authentic Christian vision for human life in this time of explosive technological change and incendiary anti-Christian attitudes and cultural patterns.

The authors originally addressed their presentations to a conference of 300 Christian pastoral leaders, scholars, and activists entitled "Allies for Faith and Renewal," held in Ann Arbor, Michigan, in May 1985. The meeting was sponsored by the Center for Pastoral Renewal, which is an outreach of an international, ecumenical Christian community called The Sword of the Spirit. The results of two previous conferences sponsored by the Center in 1980 and 1982 have been published as *Christianity Confronts Modernity* and *Summons to Faith and Renewal*.

The authors of this book hold strongly to different theological positions and are loyal to separate church bodies. How, then, can they work together? Even though they face common challenges, what have Mennonites to do with Eastern Orthodox, or Roman Catholics with Southern Baptists?

The de-Christianization of Western societies is a harsh light moving over the theological landscape. It puts some Christian differences in shadow while exposing obscured foundations to view. In the past, when Western societies seemed more generally Christian, it was the differences between Christian traditions that stood out most sharply. But now that Christian attitudes to family, sex, personal morality, and the dignity of human life are receding in the West, the common core of Christian teaching in these areas stands out more obviously. The division between the Eastern and Western churches and the Reformation cleavage seem less fundamental in an age when the entire Christian message is being resymbolized to fit secular presuppositions and political ideologies. Even though differences between historic Christian traditions remain as deep as ever, they take on the appearance of family disagreements in confrontation with aggressive anti-Christian trends. Ken Wilson argues in his essay that God is allowing Christians' thought, life, and mission to be threatened in order to drive separated Christians to a realization of how substantial our shared beliefs are, and how profound is our existing relationship as *Christians*.

Our relationship is that of brothers and sisters in Christ. While we belong to different churches and hold some differing beliefs, we are all "in Christ." While disagreeing about the proper constitution of the church and about various issues regarding faith, sacraments, and so on, we can recognize one another as brothers and sisters in the Lord, estranged members of the same spiritual family. While not fully one in mind or in church membership, we are united to one Lord and are sharers of one Holy Spirit. "He who is united to the Lord becomes one spirit with him" (1 Cor 6:17); we who are united to the Lord become one spirit with him and with one another. While we must look forward to the full restoration and expression of this unity, we are already joined to one another in the Father, Son, and Holy Spirit.

The New Testament speaks of the people of the new covenant as citizens of one nation: "You are a chosen race, a royal priesthood, a holy *nation*, God's own people" (1 Pt 2:9). "You are no longer aliens in a foreign land but fellow-*citizens*

with God's people" (Eph 2:19;NEB). Despite our ecclesiastical divisions, we are compatriots. And certainly our
separate identities as Americans, Canadians, or Germans are
overshadowed by our common identity as nationals of this
holy nation.

The concrete reality of this relationship was brought home
to me recently by a phone call that came to my house. A Jewish
believer who resides in Israel was calling Christians in the
United States to say that the situation with Christians in
Lebanon was grave. Some 40,000 to 70,000 Christians were
homeless due to attacks from Shiites and Syrians in the wake of
the Israeli withdrawal from southern Lebanon. Massacres
were occurring. The Jewish believer was urgently concerned
that more Christians were in danger of being killed. The full
report was not getting into the press, and he wanted to alert
other Christians so they could spread the word.

That was an example of Christian brotherhood. An Israeli
Christian of a free church background was showing deep care
for his Maronite and Orthodox brethren in Lebanon, calling
Protestant and Catholic friends in the United States. But the
fact that such an action is so unusual highlights the weakness
of the sense of nationhood among most Christians today.
How many of us relate to the fortunes of other Christians
around the world with such a sense of solidarity? We
Christians are often passive in the face of challenges to other
members of our own people. By contrast, how great the
conviction of peoplehood shared by American Jews in regard
to the modern nation of Israel!

Allies face a common foe. What enemy galvanizes the
incipient alliance of Christians represented in this book? What
connection exists between legal threats to religious liberties
(described here by William Ball), ideological distortions of
Christian faith (probed by Donald Bloesch), and cultural
erosion of ordinary Christian living (examined by Steve
Clark)?

Certainly these all stem from secular conceptions of the

world that are hostile to divine revelation, objective truth, moral absolutes, and the biblical message of sin and redemption. These secular biases are reinforced by structures of modern society that push religious faith to the margins of public life and detach individuals from the social groupings that contribute to strength of faith. But these and other problems addressed at the Allies for Faith and Renewal conference* are connected at a deeper level. Behind individuals and social movements that resist God's purposes are spiritual powers in rebellion against him.

The apostle Paul wrote in Ephesians:

We are not contending against flesh and blood, but against the principalities, against the powers, against the world rulers of this present darkness, against the spiritual hosts of wickedness in the heavenly places. (Eph 6:12)

---

* Conference presentations not included in this volume:
Humberto Belli, "Liberation Theology and True Liberation"; Melinda Delahoyde, "Deadly Mercy: A Report on Euthanasia—Developments, Pastoral Dimensions, Strategies for Public Policy"; Bob Gallic, "Raising the Next Generation in the Christian Faith: A Community's Experience"; Theodore Jungkuntz, Theodore Stylianopoulos, and William Kurz, "Protestant, Orthodox, and Catholic Approaches to Scripture and the Role of Tradition"; Dick Keyes, "Where Have All the Heroes Gone?"; Mark Kinzer, "Principles for Practical Ecumenical Cooperation"; Richard Land, "Secular Culture and Christian Schools"; Connie Marshner, "The Family in Public Policy Today"; Connie Marshner, William Kirk Kilpatrick, Gladys Hunt, and Therese Cirner, "Christian Womanhood in America—Past, Present, and Future: A Pastoral Perspective"; Jane Muldoon, "Strategies for Local Church Involvement in Prolife Political Action"; John Mulloy, "Christianity and the Crisis of Western Culture: A Perspective from the Historical Writings of Christopher Dawson"; J.I. Packer, "Outflanking Biblical Authority: The Use and Abuse of Hermeneutics"; Kerry Ptacek, "Ideological Distortions in the Religious Press: A Case Study—North American Perceptions of Central America"; Joseph Sobran, "Crucial Social Issues and Christian Political Alliance"; Paul Vitz, Anne Carson Daly, Bruce Longstreth, and Stephen Clark, "Christian Manhood in America—Past, Present and Future: Pastoral Perspectives"; Virgil Vogt, Alexander Webster, Philip Lawler, and Harold O.J. Brown, "Christian Positions on the Morality of War and Nuclear Weapons"; Curt Young, "Strategies for Local Church Involvement in Prolife Direct Action—Problem Pregnancy Counseling and Direct Aid".

Any alliance of Christians against contemporary notions and schemes that are leading people away from God must reckon on dealing with more than misguided theories in the professional journals or slogans in the mass media. We are engaged in a spiritual battle. The devil himself and his armies oppose the cause of Christ.

The New Testament consistently teaches that there is more evil in the world than can be attributed to human perversity. The evil in the world originates not only in men and women but also in a powerful, malicious spiritual person who hates God and seeks the destruction of the human race. Jesus called him the prince of this world. Paul called him the prince of the power of the air. John wrote, "We know that we are of God and that the whole world is in the power of the evil one." What is he like? Jesus tells us that he is a murderer, the father of lies, a thief who comes only to destroy. It was to free man from his dominion that the eternal Word came into the world. John tells us, "The reason the Son of God appeared was to destroy the works of the devil" (1 Jn 3:8). Thus, if we lose sight of the reality of Satan, we are no longer able to understand the purpose of Christ's incarnation and atonement.

Are we embarrassed by this belief? Has our thinking been so secularized that we have a blind spot for this central aspect of Christ's work? Do we maintain our formal assent to historic Christian teaching on the reality of Satan and his spiritual cohort, but without any active sense that we ourselves are engaged in spiritual warfare?

If so, we cut ourselves off from the New Testament understanding of the world. We fail to appropriate a key lesson of Scripture concerning the conflict we are in. Indeed, we are in the contradictory position of opposing the secularization of Christian faith while allowing a secularized viewpoint to blind us to the spiritual forces that lie behind that secular worldview. We must decide which will determine our thinking: the teaching and practice of Jesus and the apostles, or the secularized mindset of our age?

C.S. Lewis wrote that in times past it was Satan's strategy to manifest his works in order to intimidate, but in the modern period his policy is to conceal his work, to make it invisible to men and women with a scientific, secularized, rationalized worldview. He works most freely and effectively when we mistakenly attribute all his works to other sources. How can Christians effectively combat him if we do not recognize his existence?

In recent years, Catholic popes have warned modern Christians not to lose sight of the reality of Satan. Pope Paul VI said in 1972:

> The evil which exists in the world is the result and effect of an attack upon us and our society by a dark and hostile agent, the devil. Evil is not only a negation but a living, spiritual, corrupt and corrupting being—a terrible reality, mysterious and frightening. The testimony of both Bible and church tells us that people refuse to acknowledge his existence, or they make of him a self-subsistent principle not originating in God, unlike all creatures; or he is explained away as a pseudoreality, a fantastic personification of the unknown grounds of evil within us. . . . The devil is the enemy number one, the source of all temptation. Thus we know that this dark and destructive being really exists and is still active; he is the sophistical perverter of man's moral equipoise, the malicious seducer who knows how to penetrate us—through the senses, the imagination, desire, utopian logic, or disordered social contacts—in order to spread error. (Nov. 15, 1972)

What else, besides the presence of Satan and his evil spirits, adequately explains the depth and extent of evil that has broken forth in this century:

—the concentration camps of Nazi Germany, Soviet Russia, and Communist Cambodia?

—the practice of abortion worldwide, which has taken more human lives since World War II than all the wars in history?
—the decadence of the West, infected with divorce, promiscuity, pornography, and perversion?
—versions of the Christian message, stripped of everything transcending human reason and political programs, which close the way for millions to hear the gospel that leads to life?

The devil carries out his wicked designs not only on a large scale but also seeks to ruin individuals' lives and our modest collective efforts at doing good. He tempts us to sin, to lose faith, to lose heart. He sows suspicion, anger, rivalry, gossip, and slander in our parishes and communities, prolife and evangelistic organizations, and theological faculties. Which of us has not seen it happen?

If Christ our king is at war with a spiritual enemy, then we, his people, are unavoidably a nation at war. Whether we acknowledge it or not, Satan and his army of fallen angels, domineering over every part of human society that does not acknowledge Christ as Lord, form a kingdom at odds with Christ's kingdom, a kingdom locked in a death struggle with the kingdom of light. Whatever our service in the cause of Christ—whether it is preaching the gospel or offering anti-abortion counseling or confronting the spirit of the age in theology or simply maintaining Christian family life—we are thrust into spiritual warfare.

Although we may find the New Testament report of the spiritual battle disconcerting and unpleasant, it is not ultimately bad news. To the people of the first century and of cultures even of our own day who have not doubted the existence of evil spirits, the gospel has appeared immediately as good news. It has brought freedom from fear. For those of us who rationalistically deny the mysterious reality of evil spiritual powers, the New Testament revelation must first convince us of their existence. But after we have received the bad news, we can better appreciate the good news: Jesus Christ has overcome Satan by his death, resurrection, and ascension.

Hard warfare lies ahead of us, but the decisive battle has been fought and won, and final victory is assured. As Christian allies at this moment in history, we find ourselves on the defensive against many contemporary trends. But our alliance is not fundamentally defensive because we seek to be loyal to Christ, and he is on the offensive against his enemies. The message we have been entrusted with—the message we seek to live out, protect from distortion, and communicate to others—is a message of victory over sin and death and all the spiritual powers that wrench men and women from their God-given destiny.

Casting out demons, Christ has brought the kingdom of God upon us (Mt 12:28). Binding the strong man, Christ has broken into Satan's house and has plundered his goods (Mk 3:27). Therefore we can be confident in Christ. If we remain with him, we need have no fear, because he will not allow us to be tempted beyond our strength (1 Cor 10:13). He will give us divine help (Jas 1:5; Mt 10:19-20). If we follow him, our commander-in-chief, we can be sure that he will use us to bring down spiritual strongholds (2 Cor 10:3-5; Mt 16:18-19). We will see his complete conquest of Satan and will share in his kingdom of peace and righteousness, justice and truth.

Because we are in a *spiritual* battle, we must fight spiritually. Our trust should not be in strategies or numbers, clever litigation or use of media, organizational talents or intellectual resources. The battle is the Lord's, so our trust and hope must be in him. In the passage already referred to, Paul instructs us about spiritual conflict:

> Be strong in the Lord and in the strength of his might. Put on the whole armor of God, that you may be able to stand against the wiles of the devil. . . . Therefore take the whole armor of God, that you may be able to withstand in the evil day, and having done all, to stand. Stand, therefore, having

girded your loins with truth, and having put on the
breastplate of righteousness, and having shod your feet with
the equipment of the gospel of peace; besides all these,
taking the shield of faith, with which you can quench all the
flaming darts of the evil one. And take the helmet of
salvation, and the sword of the Spirit, which is the word of
God. Pray at all times in the Spirit, with all prayer and
supplication. To that end keep alert with all perseverance,
making supplication for all the saints. (Eph 6:10-11, 13-18)

The key to spiritual warfare is union with Christ—being
"strong in the Lord and in the strength of his might." The
armor we are to put on is his own character—"righteousness."
All the parts of the armor mentioned in the passage are
mentioned in the Old Testament as parts of the armor of the
Lord and of his Messiah when he goes forth to battle (Is 11:5;
59:17; Ps 35:2; 7:12); thus the passage directs us to be united
with the Lord as he goes into battle, united with his power, his
Spirit.

The passage refers to two offensive weapons. First it
mentions the sword of the Spirit, which is the word of God.
This means the gospel. The gospel has tremendous power to
refute error and to change men and women. We should recall it
often and declare it at every opportunity, whatever our
particular role of service. The second offensive weapon is
prayer. This too is for all of us, whatever the particular
responsibilities we have in God's service. We are supposed to
pray for the success of our work. The opposition we face in the
pastoral, academic, economic, and political spheres is spiritual
at root, and so our response must be spiritual: alert, constant,
persevering prayer that overcomes the enemy. We can pray this
way with the help of the Holy Spirit.

Paul's references to the Holy Spirit in this passage on
spiritual warfare highlight the crucial importance of the Spirit
for any alliance of Christians for faith and renewal in our day.

The magnitude of the task we face in the United States and throughout the West should make us especially conscious of the truth that we can achieve nothing apart from the guidance and power of the Holy Spirit. Tremendous spiritual and social forces are working against the gospel. How can we affect the situation if we pour our efforts into projects that are not central to God's purposes or confront the challenges with mere human wisdom and endurance?

Our approach should be that of Jesus, who said that he did only what he saw the Father doing (Jn 5:19). By the gifts of the Holy Spirit, he will enable us to see where the Father is working today so that we can make ourselves available to him for accomplishing what is most important in his plans.

But more is needed than a renewed openness to the Holy Spirit's guidance. If God is allowing the troubles of the present time as an incentive to draw Christians into cooperation with one another, he is also allowing flagrant evils to drive us to put all our hope in his power and initiative. Christians who join as allies for faith and renewal should be the foremost champions of the rediscovery of the Holy Spirit as the life of the church. Certainly, by faith and baptism Christians have already received the Holy Spirit. But have any of us yet opened our lives to all that he has come to bring? As allies, our message to the church should be that opening to the Holy Spirit is a key to responding rightly to the serious challenges of the age.

The New Testament teaches us that there is an essential connection between the coming of the Holy Spirit and the extension of God's kingdom on the earth. One such passage is the discussion between the disciples and Jesus after his resurrection, narrated in Acts:

> They asked him, "Lord, will you at this time restore the kingdom to Israel?" He said to them, "It is not for you to know times or seasons which the Father has fixed by his own authority. But you shall receive power when the Holy Spirit

has come upon you; and you shall be my witnesses in Jerusalem and in all Judea and Samaria and to the end of the earth." (Acts 1:6-9)

Jesus refused to say *when* the kingdom would be fully established. But, staying on the topic, he told the disciples *how* the kingdom was to remain among them and be extended after his ascension: they were to receive power when the Holy Spirit came on them. By the Holy Spirit they would be able to bear witness to and manifest the fact that God's kingdom was coming into the world.

The church's rapid growth and radical commitment in the period of the New Testament and the years that followed demonstrates the Spirit's powerful presence. From the Holy Spirit the Christians received boldness, courage, fervor, and wisdom to do God's will.

Because of the Holy Spirit, it was plain that God's kingdom was among them. Reading the New Testament, one is struck over and over by the manifest, obvious, almost tangible activity of the Spirit in the early Christian communities:

—Paul reminds the Thessalonians that their faith in God "has gone forth everywhere" and that they have become "an example to all the believers," because the gospel came to them "not only in word but also in power and in the Holy Spirit," and they received it "in much affliction with joy inspired by the Holy Spirit" (1 Thes 1:8, 7, 5, 6).

—The work of the Spirit in the Corinthians was apparent enough that Paul could boast to them, "You yourselves are our letter of recommendation, written on your hearts, to be known and read by all men . . . written not with ink but with the Spirit of the living God, not on tablets of stone but on tablets of human hearts" (2 Cor 3:2-3).

—The coming of the Spirit to the Galatians was so clearly observable that Paul could support a contention by asking them: "Did you receive the Spirit by works of the law, or by hearing with faith? . . . Does he who supplies the Spirit to you and works miracles among you do so by works of the law, or by hearing with faith?" (Gal 3:2-5).

The well-known passage in 1 Corinthians on the gifts of the Spirit shows us the vital link between the particular vocation and service of each Christian and the empowerment of the Spirit:

> There are varieties of gifts, but the same Spirit; and there are varieties of service, but the same Lord; and there are varieties of working, but it is the same God who inspires them all in every one. To each is given the manifestation of the Spirit for the common good. To one is given through the Spirit the utterance of wisdom, and to another the utterance of knowledge according to the same Spirit, to another faith by the same Spirit, to another gifts of healing by the one Spirit, to another the working of miracles, to another prophecy, to another the ability to distinguish between spirits, to another various kinds of tongues, to another the interpretation of tongues. All these are inspired by one and the same Spirit, who apportions to each one individually as he wills. (1 Cor 12:4-11)

Of course, this is not a complete listing of all the workings of the Spirit. The point is, however, that *all* power to bear witness to the coming of the kingdom and to build up the body of Christ comes by the Holy Spirit. The Spirit is the source, the means of God's work through us. Are we involved in forms of service to the body of Christ? Are we giving testimony to the coming of his kingdom? Then we ought to seek and expect the powerful assistance of the Spirit, who comes to accomplish through us things we could never do ourselves.

Do our churches, fellowships, and organizations experience the Holy Spirit's help? Without him, fruitfulness is choked off, endurance becomes soured by frustration, and we risk burning ourselves out. Allies for faith and renewal need access to deeper spiritual resources. We need to sink our roots into the life of God.

Sometimes the exhortation to be filled with the Holy Spirit meets with the objection that, as Christians, we already possess the Spirit. But the spiritual logic of the matter is that, if we are filled with the Spirit, all the more should we seek to be filled with him. This was certainly the view of the first Christians. We read in Acts that after Peter and John were arrested for healing a man in the name of Jesus, and were released, they gathered with the other Christians to pray.

> They lifted their voices together to God and said, "Sovereign Lord, who didst make the heaven and the earth and the sea and everything in them ... truly in this city there were gathered together against thy holy servant Jesus . . . the Gentiles and the peoples of Israel, to do whatever thy hand and thy plan had predestined to take place. And now, Lord, look upon their threats, and grant to thy servants to speak thy word with all boldness, while thou stretchest out thy hand to heal, and signs and wonders are performed through the name of thy holy servant Jesus." And when they had prayed, the place in which they were gathered together was shaken; and they were all filled with the Holy Spirit and spoke the word of God with boldness. (Acts 4:24-31)

Confronted with persecution and spiritual conflict, these believers, so recently filled with the Holy Spirit on Pentecost, sought power from God. They were mightily answered. God equipped them for the special circumstances they faced, for the particular task at hand. Similarly it is reported that at important moments the individual Christians were again "filled with the Spirit" for doing God's will in certain situations. At the end of his defense before his persecutors, Stephen, "full of the Holy Spirit," gazed into heaven and saw the glory of God (Acts 7:55). Paul, "filled with the Holy

Spirit," rebuked Elymas the magician who interfered with his preaching (Acts 13:8-10).

A constantly renewed experience of being filled with the Spirit emerges as a pattern of the early church. We see it not only in the history of Acts, but in the prayers and encouragement of Paul and the other authors of the New Testament (for example, exhortations to "Be aglow with the Spirit!" "Be filled with the Spirit." "Quench not the Spirit."—Rom 12:11; Eph 5:18; 1 Thes 5:19). This pattern is meant for our instruction. The Christian people are collectively in a global situation of grave urgency. Like the first Christians in Jerusalem, great opportunities lie before us, but we also face great opposition. As men and women engaged in spiritual warfare, we need a new filling with the Holy Spirit. The Spirit is given for boldness and wisdom and endurance, for praying and singing and rejoicing amid difficulties. The Spirit is given as a river of living water within us. Now is the time for all who are thirsty to come and drink again.

This is the tenor of some remarks by John Stott, the prominent Anglican evangelical, which speaks to all of us:

> An exhortation to us all, whatever our spiritual condition may be. Let us constantly seek to be filled with the Spirit, to be led by the Spirit, to walk in the Spirit. Can we not gladly occupy this common ground together, so that there is no division among us? Further, we can agree that the main condition of being filled is to be hungry. The Scripture tells us that God fills the hungry with good things and sends the rich empty away. "Open your mouth wide," he says, "and I will fill it" (Ps 81:10). . . . We must learn to keep coming to Jesus and to keep drinking. Only so, in the wise and balanced language of the Book of Common Prayer, shall we "daily increase in the Holy Spirit more and more, until we come into God's everlasting kingdom." (*Baptism and Fullness: The Work of the Holy Spirit Today,* pp. 74-75)

Not only the Book of Common Prayer but also the liturgies and prayers of Catholics, Orthodox, and Christians of other traditions look to God for more of the Holy Spirit.

If we seek the Holy Spirit, we must be willing to yield to his leading. The degree to which we experience the Spirit's empowerment depends not only on God's willingness but also on our faith in him and our receptivity to his working in ways that go beyond our understanding and previous experience. The range of the Spirit's activity is broader, deeper, and more powerful than we have known. Men and women accustomed to rational analysis and control may feel threatened by the gentle but strong and sovereign action of the Spirit, who blows where he wills. But if we recognize our profound need for the Holy Spirit, we will ask God to give us the faith and openness to receive him more deeply and cooperate with him in new ways. All of us who are allies for faith and renewal in the churches must make this our prayer for ourselves and for the whole Christian people.

Peter S. Williamson
Center for Pastoral Renewal

# ONE

# Threats to Religious Liberties in the Next Decade

## William B. Ball

THE AMERICAN PEOPLE are very much in court these days in cases of religious liberty, both suing and being sued by government. Perhaps the best description of what is happening in our courts now can be described by the single word, *tension*. Our people still have faith in our courts—a strong and simple faith that out there is a Constitution which will surely protect them. Also there remains among our people a strong apprehension of natural justice—the idea found in the Declaration of Independence that rights come from a Creator, rights which legislatures, courts, or even majorities cannot take away, an immutable rule which exists above the state, its courts, or even the Constitution. And we hear the counterpoint of zealous bureaucracies, calmly possessed of power, prestige, and the treasury, seemingly defending the public interest in their prosecutions, injunction proceedings, tax suits, and the rest against religious claimants.

Out of this tension come the decisions of the courts—varied, often confusing. The confusion is due in part to the mixture of good and bad decisions by the Supreme Court of the United States, which the lower courts are more or less bound to follow. That, in turn, has derived from the Supreme Court's occasional acceptance of contrived and false historical and legal theories promoted in legal briefs by various pressure groups (notably, in the cases involving religion in the public schools). The sometimes confused or plainly fallacious decisions of the Court are due also to its vulnerability to media pressures, as we saw spectacularly in the Bob Jones case, but also to serious and tragic departures from our traditions of civility—the abortion decision, *Roe* v. *Wade,* being a monstrous example of such departure.

Let me briefly sum up what the Supreme Court has laid down in the area where state and religion are in confrontation, because only in light of that can we perceive any threats to religious liberty. Here we should go chiefly to the religion clause of the First Amendment, though it is true that other provisions of the Constitution, relating to equal protection of the laws, due process, the Ninth Amendment, and even the search and seizure clause, or the Fifth Amendment's privilege against self-incrimination, may prove the constitutional terrain on which the religious liberty battle is to be fought.

The First Amendment's two religion clauses (a) protect the free exercise of religion against action by government and (b) prohibit the establishment of religion by government. Under the free exercise clause the Supreme Court has prescribed four tests which the courts are to apply when someone claims, in court, that the government is violating religious liberty: (1) Is religion really involved? (2) Does the government action really injure religion? (3) If it does, is that action nevertheless justified by a "compelling state interest"? (4) If it is so justified, can the societal objective of the government's action be achieved by other, less restrictive means? Great difficulties often arise in the application of this test. But it would seem that, no matter how hard we ponder situations in which government and religion come into conflict, we would have to wind up by asking those four questions.

A very good example of how the test works was seen in the case of *Wisconsin* v. *Yoder*. In this case, Amish parents were being criminally prosecuted for their refusal to send their children to high school. To defend these people in court, we had to address ourselves, first of all, to the question of whether the Amish refusal of high schooling was really a religious matter. Naturally the court would need to be satisfied as to that. The process of judicial inquiry must avoid giving credence to whims. Courts rightly look to the sincerity of the claimant and evidences of the reality of his belief (though not to whether it is true).

Next, the inquiry turns to whether there has been injury to the exercise of religious belief. Here it is important to stress that it is not for government to decide whether the religious claimant has been injured; that is essentially a question which only those within the faith community can answer. Nevertheless, constantly in court cases we find government attorneys asserting that some governmental action which they are defending is in no way injurious to religion. I listened to a justice of one of our state Supreme Courts recently saying that he found no religious injury in a governmental scheme to control a religious child-care institution. He stated that he was a church-going individual; how could it be that what did not offend him offended the religious claimants in the case? With respect to these *religious* issues which arise in litigations, the question always must center on: What is belief to the believer and what constitutes injury to the religious practice in the eyes of that believer?

Now, in court cases the burden of proof thereafter shifts to government. That is a point that we must realize and insist upon. Government must now show that its action is justified by a "compelling state interest" and that that interest cannot be realized by any less restrictive means than the action contemplated. It is not sufficient, therefore, that the government attorney simply inform the court that the legislature, in its wisdom, has authorized the action in question. That was what the State of Wisconsin tried to do in the *Yoder* case. The state's attorney simply pointed to the existence of the Wisconsin compulsory attendance statute and asked what more needed to be said in justification of the state's truancy action against the Amish. But the Supreme Court of the United States, in that case, said that this did not at all suffice. The state would have to *prove* that imposing that statute on the Amish was a matter of supreme, life-or-death necessity. When we speak of "compelling state interest," we are not talking about a mere "public" interest. No, we are speaking of a supreme interest. Such compelling state interest, the Supreme Court ruled, was not evident in the *Yoder* case, and the court decided in favor of the parents.

Religious liberty has had some very supportive decisions from the Supreme Court in the past, as well as a number of decisions which are negative and constrictive. In looking ahead to the future, I would make the following comments.

For one thing, I think it may be true that the heyday of a liberal interpretation of the Bill of Rights has, for the time, passed. In the 1940s, '50s, '60s, and '70s, the Supreme Court made very generous readings of the Bill of Rights, some very much to the benefit of religious liberty but mostly in the fields of crime, pornography, and national security. In those three areas, state laws enacted to protect the public were repeatedly overthrown by the Supreme Court. This was certainly climaxed in the preposterous and malevolent decision in 1973 striking down state abortion statutes. Not surprisingly, we now find a reaction setting in against those decisions, some of which were certainly very damaging to the protection of the public interest. Now, however, we are not witnessing a carry-over in *religion* cases. I see two trends.

The *first* is an almost angry reaction against the extravagances of the courts in the past three decades. The new conservatism shifts emphasis from the judiciary to the legislature. At least that has been so in religion cases. The view now taken as "conservative" holds that the legislature is the true organ of democracy, the branch of government most readily responsive to the people, and hence the judgments of the legislature ought not be reviewed by the courts except in the most extreme cases. This is a Benthamite view of law, precluding questioning whether there are natural rights, as given, for example, in the Bill of Rights, which even the legislature may not be suffered to abridge. However, with regard to this view of legislative supremacy, we must point out, *in fact*, especially in sensitive areas of social and educational legislation, it is frequently the case today that you do not get a legislative judgment. Rather, the legislative hearings come to be dominated by highly credentialed experts acting on behalf of groups which have their own peculiar social programs to enact. Legislators often find themselves quite overpowered by the experts, who appear to have an almost encyclopedic knowledge of what they are talking about and who—cocksure—present voluminous though often problematic research documents. Further, the legislator who is not too energetic or bright will not find unwelcome the fact that apparently skillfully drafted legislation is presented to him, prefab, ready to go, and backed by such impressive scholarship. Often, too, these pressure groups' legislative efforts are convoyed in public opinion by sympathetic media. Finally—and this is especially significant—religious groups very often have no lobby, no political clout, no propaganda machine, and no money with which to carry forward such efforts.

The end result of the legislative effort, therefore, may be that laws are enacted inimical to religion or particular religious interests. Yet, under the foregoing supposedly "conservative" doctrine, the court will deem the legislative effort as the "will of the people" and never question it— though it may be the last thing in the world which "the people" would desire if they knew what it was all about.

The **second** trend which I see is the tendency to regard religious liberty as an afterthought. Courts are increasingly tending to say that the public interest, represented by a certain law, is more important than religious liberty. Religious liberty must wait its turn. It is obvious that virtually all laws which are enacted are in the public interest. Laws in the field of environment, national defense, crime, zoning, etc., are invariably truly in the public interest. But that does not mean that they may be applied to constrict First Amendment liberties where those liberties are proved to exist. That is where, if the Constitution is really to be followed, the First Amendment liberty must be given very heavy weight when placed in the balancing scales. If it is to be outweighed, it must be outweighed only in those relatively few applications of public interest that are crucial to the existence of society.

Let me now briefly mention another aspect of our liberties as given in the religion clauses of the First Amendment. I refer to the prohibition against an "establishment of religion." That phrase was adopted, of course, in the interest of preventing the setting up of a governmental church in this country. Long since, the phrase has been otherwise interpreted by the Supreme Court, but that is a lengthy tale which I will not attempt to address here. However, one aspect of that interpretation pertains to what the Supreme Court has called "excessive entanglement." Since 1970 the Court has been stressing that laws calling for actions that involve government too extensively in the affairs of religious bodies are forbidden by the First Amendment's establishment clause. While no historic justification exists for the "excessive entanglement" doctrine, the doctrine is probably salutary when applied to religious liberty cases. In other words, the doctrine protects against governmental surveillance, inspection, auditing, day-to-day relationships, or any aspect of governance of religious bodies by the state.

What areas pose particular threats to religious liberty at this hour? I see them as the following:

**1. The right to bear Christian witness in education.** This is a supremely important area. It is also an area of intense conflict. During the past decade cases have been coming to the courts in which it was plain that the state sought to control religious freedom in education. The National Labor Relations Board sought to impose its own jurisdiction over Catholic schools in Illinois, Indiana, and Pennsylvania in the 1970s. Happily, this effort was beaten back in the courts.

The cases that are on the cutting edge of religious liberty in our country today involve fundamentalist and evangelical schools. In Michigan, what is perhaps the most important religious liberty case in the United States will be argued before the Michigan Supreme Court. This is the *Sheridan Road Baptist Church* case, involving state control of teachers and curriculum in religious schools, and requiring state licensing of religious ministries in education. Two very excellent and courageous fundamentalist Christian churches, Sheridan Road Baptist Church and First Baptist Church, have resisted these government controls by suing the State of Michigan. They prevailed in the trial court, their victory was reversed by the Michigan Court of Appeals, and now they are pinning their hopes on the Supreme Court of Michigan. Theirs is a very basic case on the free exercise of religion and with respect to forbidden entanglements between state and church.

**2. Religious liberty in public education.** In 1963 the religion of secular humanism became officially installed, pursuant to a United States Supreme Court decision, in the public schools of our country. Our public schools have had to deal with the lives and emotions and attitudes of children, their many problems, their fears, their morals, and their hopes—all from perspectives which must exclude the acknowledgment of God and the presenting of God-centered morality in any affirmative way. The universal moral crisis in our land is, of course, the direct product of this kind of education.

Also, however, there has not been a mere absence of God-centered teaching; there has also been the addition of specifically secular humanist programs, especially in areas relating to values and attitude. So, for example, in Michigan there are now programs relating to sex, to globalism, and to many other areas which closely relate to the child's attitude toward his own conduct and toward the world. These are flatly unconstitutional impositions. They are loaded with danger to our liberties in the future.

**3. Taxation of ministries.** In the case of *Bob Jones University* v. *United States,* the Supreme Court held that in order to be tax exempt, a religious institution must conform to "federal public policy." Exemption from taxation is economically necessary to nonprofit institutions of religion. The court's ruling will thus be extremely burdensome when an institution, for religious reasons, *cannot* conform to a certain "public policy." You can easily see the extreme evil which this view represents. It has nothing to do with the Constitution. In fact, it contradicts the Constitution. Who is going to determine what is meant by "federal public policy"? We have federal public policy with respect to the environment, national defense, and many other areas. Here, religious bodies must be allowed breathing room to hold to views which some may feel are opposed to "public policy." That is of the essence, as I see it.

There are certainly those who today advocate a "public policy" of population control. If a religious institution maintains and teaches to the contrary, shall it lose its tax exempt status? It shall, if the court merely says that population control represents "federal public policy." This is nothing other than the Nazi doctrine of *Gleichshaltung*: all activity must be coordinated to the ends of the state.

Under this heading of taxation of ministries, we also see efforts now being made, for the first time in our history, to tax churches. In 1983 and 1984 the Social Security Act was amended by Congress to provide, for the first time, for the taxation of churches—this under the Social Security Act. This is flagrantly unconstitutional, and I am happy to report that the constitutional issue will be aired presently in our courts in a case known as *Bethel Baptist Church* v. *United States of America.*

**4. Denial of religious advocacy in politics.** Already in the tax exemption section of the Internal Revenue Code known as Section 501(c)(3), there is a limitation on political activity of religious groups. The constitutionality of that limitation has never been tested in the Supreme Court. Perhaps more significant is the fact that there are pressure groups that have militantly advocated that churches and church leaders be barred from entering the political arena and from making political comment.

I am sure that, in this connection, you are aware of the Mario Cuomo school of religious restraint (at least restraint on Cuomo-selected issues such as abortion). The Supreme Court itself, in the *Lemon* case, in 1971, warned against activities that create "political division along religious lines." That is dangerous thinking, and unconstitutional thinking. We have a great and commendable history of religious "intervention" in politics. The American people are always able to resist bad advocacy; we do not need the force of law in order to shut up bad religious advocates.

**5. Denial of the religious right of sexual differentiation.** Keep an eye on the case known as *Dayton Christian Schools* v. *Ohio Civil Rights Commission.* That case involves a religious body, required by its theology to sexually differentiate, and a female member of that religious body. The member had accepted employment with that differentiation as a condition but then dissented and was discharged. The member is now suing the religious body on the grounds of sex discrimination. It is plain that the religious body had a *constitutional* right to sexually differentiate according to its theology, and that the female employee came into the employment with full knowledge of the doctrine in question. The federal district court in that case, however, held that the religious principle must be set aside in view of the allegations of sex discrimination—a remarkably bad decision. The U.S. Court of Appeals for the Sixth Circuit reversed the lower court's decision, and the state has now appealed to the U.S. Supreme Court. I see the sex-discrimination area as one that contains serious problems with respect to religious liberty.

**6. Denial of the right to separateness of the faith community.** There are apparently those in our society who are uneasy with religious liberty. They desire to religiously homogenize society. I do not speak here of ecumenism; rather, I speak of the pressure of those who would require religion to become an ineffectual and nondistinctive force in our society.

In the province of Alberta, Canada, a thoroughly incredible public document has been produced through the efforts of various pressure groups that would create state-enforced "Guidelines on Tolerance and Understanding." This is right out of George Orwell. The government would come into schools throughout the province, including religious schools, and audit them according to a check list relating to tolerance and understanding. I think you can readily see that a good deal of teaching from the gospels would have to go by the boards under such a program. We have to look very carefully at some of the group defamation statutes now in the works in many state legislatures. Fortunately or unfortunately, the right of religious expression embraces the right of religious difference. We must beware of pleas given in the name of "tolerance" which would in fact result in governmental intolerance through the suppression of teaching based upon doctrine. In the same connection, we must beware of the introduction of programs under labels implying "tolerance" which are intended to shape attitudes towards groups which may run contrary to one's scriptural teaching.

What is to be done about these threats to religious liberty?

First, and most obviously, we must muster the courage of our duty of witness. The first place where religious liberty is lost is in the lukewarmness of people who profess religion. We have to decide where our treasure lies. Once we have that decision in hand, we will then do our duty courageously in order to defend religious rights.

Second, I see the need for a charitable and humble willingness to stand together. Again, I am not speaking of an ecumenism that would seek to blend differences of belief. Rather, to mention but one example, I see a marvelous consistency between the views of fundamentalists, Catholics, and many evangelicals on the abortion question. On this, and many other issues, we have a common moral position, indeed a common theological position. Why cannot we cooperate with one another in opposing evil or in promoting the good? Third, we must reverse the ongoing secularization of religion. The loss of religious liberty is closely tied to the whole matter of the secularizing of religion.

Fourth, it is time to bear witness sacrificially. Religious groups must eschew public funding wherever any significant public controls would accompany such funding. I quite realize that, in its pursuit of justice, the state may seem to furnish various benefits to religion. The familiar example of police and fire protection of churches comes at once to mind, but also such programs as benefit children, which may ultimately redound to the benefit of religious institutions, such as busing or forms of health protection or auxiliary educational services. Yet there is reason for very active concern that religious bodies not permit their ability to act sacrificially to be destroyed through dependency upon government.

Fifth, we should avoid silly and irrational approaches in court cases. I have noticed some attacks on judges and the judicial system in general which give the impression that the objectors are really against the American system of government and which create the notion that the judiciary is in the total grip of the devil. I do not think the grip is total. We ought to avoid the religious coercion of judges.

Finally, we should utilize the law. We are still a free society, and we ought to use all the civil weaponry available to us in fighting our battles. We have not gone under, and if we resist statism intelligently we shall not go under.

I close with words which I seem to recall from *Les Miserables* of Victor Hugo: "There must be some who pray always for those who pray never." We must always labor courageously for those of our brothers and sisters who know not the peril. We owe to those who differ with us kindness and candor, but we do not owe them obedience. Our obedience instead is to Christ. It is with him, ultimately, rather than by courts and attorneys, that our struggles will be won.

# TWO

# God's Strategy for Overcoming Our Parochialism

*Ken Wilson*

AN AWFUL THING HAPPENED to the apple of God's eye in 935 B.C. God judged his people by dividing them. This people, which God had sovereignly joined together by covenant, was torn asunder. Israel was divided into a northern kingdom and a southern kingdom—a rupture that was never repaired.

The tragedy began to unfold with Solomon. He ruled a united kingdom at the zenith of Israel's earthly glory, but in his later years, under the influence of his many wives, he turned to idolatry. God spoke to Solomon prophetically, warning him of judgment on his house—the division in his kingdom. God foretold that he would tear out ten tribes from his kingdom and give them over to one of Solomon's servants.

The fulfillment of these prophecies followed Solomon's death. His son Rehoboam, who succeeded him, turned out to be just the man to provoke division. He treated the northern tribes more harshly than his father had, and they rebelled against him.

From 935 B.C. until 721 B.C., when the northern kingdom fell to the Assyrian armies, God's people in the two kingdoms were afflicted with a parochial spirit. Narrowness limited their vision. As never before, they became preoccupied with life in their own backyard, little concerned for their brothers and sisters across the border.

Yet brothers and sisters they remained, in God's eyes. He continued to address them as "brethren" of one another. At the time of the break, the prophet Shemaiah announced to Rehoboam: "Thus says the Lord, You shall not go up or fight against your brethren, the people of Israel" (1 Kgs 12:24). Years later, the prophet Oded declared to warriors of the northern kingdom after their conquest of an army of Judah: "Send back the captives of your brethren whom you have taken, for the fierce wrath of the Lord is upon you" (2 Chr 28:11).

In context the term "brethren" was not a mere figure of speech. It had all the content of the duties of the law given to Israel. To be "brethren" was to have a profound responsibility to help one another, to aid one another in times of military danger or economic hardship, to deal with each other justly, to rejoice together in prosperity, and to mourn together in suffering. But the parochial spirit with which God's people of north and south repudiated these obligations of "brethren" was epitomized in the northern tribes' parting words at the moment of their division from the tribe of Judah and the house of David: "When all Israel saw that the king of Judah did not listen to them, the people answered the king saying, 'What portion do we have in David? We have no inheritance in the son of Jesse. To your tents, O Israel; now look after your own house, David'" (1 Kgs 12:16).

"Look after your own house"—the phrase reminds me of something my friends and I would say years ago playing softball in Detroit. In the absence of a regular diamond, we would play in the street. The houses were fairly close to the street, and most of them had a big bay window in the front.

The situation taught you to hit up the middle, because if you hit to the right or to the left, you were liable to break one of those windows. Before every game, we would shout out: "No chips on windows," meaning we would not go together to pay for damages if someone broke a window. You were on your own if you broke one of those windows. Take care of your own business. Look after your own house. If you find yourself in need, look elsewhere. What concern do we have for you?

It does not take profound insight to see that a parochial spirit, a narrow vision, a disinclination to look after the well-being of brothers and sisters beyond the borders of our own church communion afflicts the Christian people today. Take the recent case of the Egyptian patriarch. Some months ago the Coptic Church appealed to Christians around the world to observe a day of prayer for the release of her leader, Pope Shenouda, who was under house arrest by the Egyptian government. Though there seem to be indications of a significant evangelical renewal in the Coptic church, though the Coptic church is one of the few slender plantings of the faith in the Middle East that has any opportunity to give testimony to the message of Jesus Christ, how many evangelical Protestants in their Sunday services joined in prayer for the release of Pope Shenouda? How many even knew about it? Or take the case of the Central American evangelical head of state, Rios Montt. He became president of Guatemala through a military coup. As with all the news from Central America, for months there were conflicting reports as to whether his regime was better or worse than that of his predecessor, and whether it was Christian or not. But there was enough evidence of his personal sincerity about bringing biblical principles to bear that we might at least wonder what opportunities were lost by his ouster, which, it seems, was made easier by the traditional animosity and lack of cooperation between Roman Catholics and Protestants in that country. Look after your own house, Egyptian Orthodox. Take care of your own business. If you find yourself in need, Guatemalan evangelicals, look elsewhere. What concern do we have for you?

Consider this present ecumenical conference. The fact that it is extraordinary for Orthodox, Protestant, Pentecostal, Roman Catholic, and Jewish Christians to gather with the view of sharing what they have learned about common cultural challenges in the United States should be a source of embarrassment to us. The fact that it occurs so seldom suggests how deeply afflicted the Christian people—we ourselves—are with a parochial spirit, a limitation of concern.

Our restricted perspective is deeply rooted. The problem is beyond the reach of the good intentions of the leaders of the Christian people to change; beyond the reach of gestures of reconciliation, as welcome and appropriate as those may be; beyond the reach of theological commissions and dialogues, no matter how helpful. "Unless the Lord builds the house, those who build it labor in vain" (Ps 127:1). Unless the Lord intervenes in the history of his people, there is no hope that we will recognize one another as "brethren."

If we look for signs of God's intervention, what can we see? What is God doing to stretch our vision, to widen our hearts? What is he doing to provoke his people to work together on the basis of what they already have in common? I believe he is doing three things.

First of all, God is pouring out his Spirit in a wide variety of churches in an unprecedented way. I am not referring only to the Pentecostal movement or the charismatic renewal but to a revival of the life of God among his people. In the Roman Catholic church there are movements such as Oasis (in Poland), the Focolare (in Italy and elsewhere), the Cursillo (in Spain and elsewhere). Among Protestants there are movements such as Campus Crusade for Christ, Youth with a Mission, the Navigators. There are countless missionary initiatives and charitable works. In movements, organizations, and churches we are seeing deep conversions to the Lord Jesus, love for God's word, good works inspired by God. One of the reasons God is doing all this, I believe, is to bear convincing testimony to us of his presence in unexpected places.

Peter's growing understanding of who was invited to the messianic banquet provides a biblical paradigm for understanding God's strategy to break down parochialism. At the outset, Peter was as narrow in his concerns as the worst of us. Simply, he expected the reign of God to come to the Jews alone. Peter, presumably, was one of the disciples who urged Jesus to send away the Syrophoenician woman who was pestering him—why bother with a gentile woman? (Mt 7:24-30) Jesus' response to the woman did not burn Peter's ears as it does the modern-day gentile reader's. After his resurrection, when Jesus said to him: "Peter, feed my sheep" (Jn 21:15-17), Peter thought he knew who the sheep were: Jews, of course! Indeed, the sheep at that point *were* mostly Jews—mostly Galileans known to Peter personally.

But after Pentecost, the words "feed my sheep" came back to haunt Peter. As people came into the church in batches of three thousand and five thousand in a single day—and not just Galilean Jews but also Hellenistic Jews, and Jews from all the provinces of the Roman empire—Peter was stretched beyond his narrow perspective. "Feed my sheep" was a bigger job than Peter first imagined. Later, God called Peter to visit the house of Cornelius and the men and women who were gathered in his living room. They were gentiles. When Jesus said, "Feed my sheep," Peter had no idea that he was talking about gentile sheep as well as Jewish ones. The idea that God would work in the lives of gentiles by his Holy Spirit was revolutionary for Peter. His amazement is apparent in his account to the brethren in Jerusalem of how he went to Cornelius's house and what happened there—an account in which Peter is trying to make sense of the inexplicable thing that has happened, for which he has no theological framework for understanding. He describes how God clearly arranged the meeting: the vision of the unclean animals which occurred three times, the man coming just then to invite him to go to Cornelius's house, and the sense of freedom he had to go there. Then he says:

> "As I began to speak, the Holy Spirit came on them as he had come on us at the beginning. Then I remembered what the Lord had said: 'John baptized with water, but you will be baptized with the Holy Spirit.' So if God gave them the same gift as he gave us who believed in the Lord Jesus Christ, who was I to think that I could oppose God?" When they [the church leaders in Jerusalem] heard this, they had no further objections, and praised God saying: "So then, God has even granted the gentiles repentance unto life."
> (Acts 11:15-18)

Would that we all had such discernment.

Remember, Peter enjoyed three years of flesh-and-blood discipleship with the Lord Jesus. He had forty days of personal instruction from the risen Christ about the kingdom of God. And yet Peter did not have a broad enough vision of God's purposes to enable him to understand the inclusion of the gentiles in the people of God. God did not woo Peter out of his parochial perspective, giving him years of reflection and the mellowing of age to bring him to the understanding that the gentiles were to be part of the kingdom of God. God forced Peter's hand. He gave Peter evidence so convincing that Peter, as a man of integrity, could not deny that God was at work in gentiles and that gentiles were now becoming, through the Lord Jesus, his brothers and his sisters.

Vinson Synan, the assistant general superintendent of the Pentecostal Holiness Church, one of the oldest Pentecostal churches in the country, grew up in the midst of intense animosity between Pentecostals and Roman Catholics. I have heard him tell of carrying into adulthood some deeply negative views. But the day came when God forced his hand. Synan describes how he visited a gathering of Roman Catholics involved in the Catholic charismatic renewal in a stadium at the University of Notre Dame a dozen years ago. As he experienced the worship in the assembly, he began to weep. He wept at the reality of God's presence among Roman Catholics, which to him was a wonder. He wept also at the beauty of the Pentecostal worship among these Roman Catholic people. God was bearing credible testimony to this Pentecostal man of his presence in this group of Roman Catholics.

When Peter saw the Holy Spirit fall on gentiles in Cornelius's living room, the revelation brought with it a solemn responsibility. Up to that time, Peter could with a clear conscience ignore gentiles. But once he had received divine testimony of God's presence among them, he had to begin to think about caring for them. Peter did not have to become a gentile himself, but woe to him if he failed to feed those sheep! Woe to him if he failed to reach out to them as brothers and sisters.

If God is graciously bearing witness to his presence in unexpected places, his purpose is to break us out of the limited perspective that has been born of the division of our churches and nurtured by our own clannishness. Like Peter, we must not fail to care for those to whom God has clearly given his Holy Spirit.

Second, God is at work to break down our parochial mindset by offering us his life and help through brothers and sisters in other Christian communions. We can learn some lessons about this from Paul's discussion of Jews and gentiles in his letter to the Romans. He gave hints there of God's strategy for uniting Jewish and gentile believers, but what he says throws light on relationships between Catholic, Protestant, and Orthodox as well. Paul is addressing a church which is increasingly composed of gentile believers. Only a few years before, the church was grappling with the problem of how to make room for a few gentiles; now the church is becoming dominated by gentiles. Paul speaks about the mystery of the Jewish people's temporary lack of response to the message of the Messiah. Paul says that God's work among the gentiles will provoke the Jewish people to a redemptive envy: "Salvation has come to the gentiles to make Israel envious" (Rom 11:11). God has set up a humbling scenario for many Jewish people: the first will be last and the last will be first. The Jewish people, the bearers of the messianic light, the first to be offered the gospel, will be the last to receive the gospel in fullness. "Israel has experienced the hardening in part until the full number of gentiles has come in, and so all Israel shall be saved" (Rom 11:25-26). In practice, this means that many Jewish people will receive the knowledge of the Messiah from gentile believers in the Lord Jesus.

The story of a friend of mine is not untypical. His grandfather was a Talmudic scholar, and his father is the president of a synagogue. He himself came to friendship with the God of Abraham, Isaac, and Jacob in large part through the help of some white, Anglo-Saxon Protestants—nice people, mind you, but gentiles. There were also some Jewish believers who helped him over the hump, but it was the white, Anglo-Saxon Protestants who played a key part in his return to God through the Messiah. This was humbling. His story, in some fashion, is the story of countless other Jewish believers, who have received the life of the God of Israel through and from gentile believers.

But Paul also goes to even greater lengths in Romans 9 to 11 to remind the gentile brethren that they have received life through the Jewish people. He reminds the gentile believers of the privileges of Israel: theirs is the adoption as sons, theirs is the divine glory, theirs is the covenant, the law, the worship of the temple, the promises, the patriarchs, and the human ancestry of Christ. The rejection of the gospel by Israel has brought untold blessing to the gentiles, and Israel's acceptance of the gospel in the final phase of God's plan will bring even greater blessing. If the Jews' "transgression means riches for the world, and their loss means riches for the gentiles, how much greater riches will their fullness bring?" (Rom 11:12).

He is warning the gentile believers not to adopt a condescending attitude toward Jews.

Paul is using a simple strategy here to unite Jewish and gentile believers: Don't bite the hand that feeds you. Remember from whom you received the life of God, for which you should be so grateful. God has arranged the process of redemption in such a way that the gentiles have received the gospel from the Jewish people, and many of the Jewish people will receive the gospel from gentile brothers and sisters. Both must profoundly humble themselves to receive life from a spoon they might otherwise consider unworthy.

Very likely, I believe, we will see similar measures used by God to bring Orthodox, Protestants, Pentecostals, Roman Catholics, and Jewish believers to walk together as brothers and sisters in mutual support in spite of their differences. In his providence, God is arranging for us to receive life from each other in order to bind us together.

My background, as may be clear by now, is strongly Protestant. My great-grandfather was a member of the Ulster Constabulary. Many of my ancestors were Plymouth Brethren. My early Christian formation as an adult came from a man who belonged to the Ceylon Pentecostal Mission (they were sending missionaries to the United States). I was associated with a Christian fellowship in Detroit that was so fearful of institutionalization that it took them sixteen years to formally appoint elders. But I have received untold grace and help from God through Roman Catholic believers.

For example, a few years ago I was working too hard and not paying enough attention to my wife and children. My wife and I got together with a Catholic member of our community here in Ann Arbor, a man who has been our friend and who has taken pastoral concern for us. He asked my wife, "Nancy, how do you think things are going?" Nancy, whom God has blessed with honesty, replied, "Well, I think there are some problems that need attention." Our friend helped us identify the problems and agree on what we would do about them. The grace of God for our marriage was imparted to us through him.

I am not in the habit of quoting statements by the Vatican, but the following passage from the Second Vatican Council's "Decree on Ecumenism" expresses the willingness to receive from other Christians which I believe God is calling us to have:

> Catholics must joyfully acknowledge and esteem the truly Christian endowments from our common heritage which are to be found among separated brethren. It is right and salutary to recognize the riches of Christ and virtuous works in the lives of others who are bearing witness to Christ, sometimes even to the shedding of their blood, for God is always wonderful in his works and worthy of admiration. Nor should we forget that whatever is wrought by the Holy Spirit in the hearts of our separated brethren can contribute to our own edification.

The Roman Catholic church has a very high view of the resources that have been deposited within her by God. Yet we have here an acknowledgement that Catholics ought to be built up by the life of God in other Christian communions. Many of our churches stand in need of wisdom and experience that fellow Christians in other churches have gained as they have proclaimed and demonstrated the kingdom, pastored, taught, and lived in the context of our secular culture. In showing us this, God is motivating us to build bridges of flesh and blood between divided church communions.

In the years ahead many of us will find ourselves in a position of personal need—for help, encouragement, spiritual strength, wisdom, money, public support in a time of criticism. In God's providence, the help may not always be offered from our own backyard; it may only be available to us from someone else's backyard. God is not afraid to pressure us. He will bring many of us to a point where our well-being depends on receiving life from Christians in other churches.

If we humble ourselves we will receive the help we need.

Finally, God is seeking to deliver us from parochialism through the fierce attacks that he is allowing to fall on the Christian churches throughout the world. Many of us will not begin to cooperate with fellow Christians in other churches primarily out of a desire to foster unity. The concerns of our hearts are different from the concerns of his heart; we are not as pained as he is at the divisions among his people. We don't see the divisions as a sign of his judgment on the whole church and a call to repent. However, we are beginning to realize that the same forces that undermine faith in our own backyards are at work in the backyards of other people, and that we may be able to learn something from one another and help one another.

The British and the Free French were allies during World War II. The alliance did not come about because Winston Churchill and Charles de Gaulle were good buddies. As a matter of fact, de Gaulle drove Churchill to distraction, and Churchill said that "the heaviest cross I have to bear is the Cross of Lorraine"—referring to the symbol of the Free French forces. Yet the British and the Free French stood with one another and risked their lives together because they faced a common enemy. Despite their mutual antipathy, Churchill could weep when he heard de Gaulle's radio announcement on the day of the Normandy invasion.

The homeowner living in a row of adjoining condominiums who discovers that one of his neighbors has termites will go to the condominium association meeting that week, not necessarily out of any great love for his neighbor but certainly out of a desire to preserve his own property. He will be willing to give his neighbor all the advice and help he can, and he will pitch in to a common fund for extermination services because he knows that his neighbor's termites are eating their way to his own unit.

Thus, we who have come to this conference have nothing to be proud of. In a sense, God is forcing us into this. In a world where Western materialistic secularism, Marxism, and a resurgent Islam are challenging the faith all over the world, God is taking drastic measures to bring us into alliances. God is not gently prodding the Christian people to work together; he is forcing our hand. He has placed us in an age of radical challenges and attacks on Christian belief, on the Christian way of life, and on Christian mission. He is using our common enemies to cause us to recognize believers in other church communions as our brothers and sisters. That he is dealing with us in this way is a cause for great humility among us. Our stubbornness has provoked him to employ drastic measures.

For his name's sake and for our own sake, may God grant us the grace to seize the opportunities, whatever they are, to work together. God grant us the grace to thank him for whatever measure of unity we do have, while not forgetting that there is a much greater measure that we hope to receive. Let us be faithful to the little that God has already given us as a basis for cooperation and not decry how small it is. If we are faithful in little things, we will be given more. Let us then be faithful with whatever measure of unity we have and seize opportunities to work together to glorify God's name.

# THREE

# The Crisis in Roman Catholicism: An Object Lesson for Evangelical Protestants

*James Hitchcock*

A CERTAIN CONVERGENCE BETWEEN Roman Catholics and evangelical Protestants has been one of the most important religious developments of the past decade, with a number of significant dimensions.

Even for relatively well-informed Catholics, the evangelical phenomenon has been a revelation. Used to paying little attention to Protestantism before the Second Vatican Council, afterwards Catholics were likely to make ecumenical contacts mainly among liberal Protestants, to the point where orthodox Catholics found themselves in doubt about the viability of the whole ecumenical enterprise. The belated encounter with evangelicals has opened up an entirely new ecumenical vista and has caused some Catholics to say that in fact real ecumenism—among strong, believing Christians—is barely beginning.

But a closer look at any reality is likely to bring second and third thoughts. If evangelicals were first largely invisible to Catholics, and if then they came to seem encouragingly orthodox and committed in their faith, still further acquaintance suggests that evangelicalism is not free of the problems which have plagued Roman Catholicism during the past two decades. If ecumenism partly means learning from one another, it can perhaps be suggested that one of the things which evangelicals can learn from Catholics is not to make the same mistakes (a lesson, it must be admitted, many Catholics failed to learn from liberal Protestants).

Obviously, the evangelical scene, like the Catholic scene, is quite diverse, so that generalizations are perilous. In addition, evangelicalism immediately poses the problem of definition—who can or should be called an evangelical? Is that phenomenon significantly different from what is called fundamentalism, and if so how? For purposes of this analysis it will perhaps suffice merely to say that certain trends here discussed do exist in certain segments of evangelicalism, even if they do not apply to the entire movement.

The Roman Catholic experience is relevant to evangelicals perhaps most of all in terms of the remarkable, indeed even amazing, speed with which religious change has occurred since the Second Vatican Council. Anyone who merely pays attention to newspaper headlines is aware, in the mid-1980s, that thousands of priests and nuns have given up their vocations in the Catholic church, that there is scarcely a single Catholic doctrine which is not attacked or challenged by some people, that a militant feminist movement is demanding radical change in the church, and that no authority—whether Scripture itself or the hierarchy of the church—is accorded full respect.

No one in 1960 could have predicted that this would happen, although in ten years' time it was fully underway. Indeed, almost all these changes, which have been rippling outwards ever since, took place in the period 1965-1970, just after the close of the Second Vatican Council.

A survey at the time[1] showed, among other things, a pattern whereby certain Catholics moved very swiftly from one position to another, often espousing dissenting positions which, only a short time before, they had assured other Catholics they had no attraction to. Some of these "leaders" actually abandoned their faith and slid swiftly into a wholly secular outlook.

Paradoxically, many of these people began by calling for a purification of their faith, for a return to a more demanding and rigorous version of it. Among some Catholics, for example, this took the form of a return to Scripture and a proclaimed intention of following as closely as possible the teachings of the New Testament. In liturgical worship, so close to the heart of Catholic piety, it was often their announced intention to recover the liturgy of the early church. Existing forms of Catholicism were often criticized for being themselves too worldly and too compromising. Rather than relying on specific rules and moral laws, for example, Catholics were told that they should spontaneously live lives of heroic virtue, motivated by nothing except the love of God.

Among many "reformers," however, this phase passed quickly. Many Catholics who "rediscovered" Scripture also learned from liberal Protestants how to "demythologize" it so as to avoid its more inconvenient teachings. Favored styles in liturgy soon came to be a mere aping of current secular fashions. Once rules had been discarded, it became apparent that those who had discarded them were now prepared to do precisely those things which the rules had previously forbidden.

The motivating force for "reform" on the part of many Catholics of the post-conciliar era eventually stood revealed as a kind of unfocused spiritual restlessness. Few of them deliberately misled their fellow Catholics as to the nature of their intentions. For the most part they simply lacked self-knowledge. Consciously, they thought that their commitment to the faith was secure, when in reality what they yearned for was a total liberation from one or other aspect of that commitment. In the process of self-discovery, and in the process of working out the demands of that restlessness, they produced a considerable upheaval in the church, which is still being felt.

As numerous Christian observers have pointed out, the secularity of modern culture is so pervasive that many Christians imbibe essentially secular ways of looking at the world without realizing it. On the everyday level this can have devastating consequences as regards, for example, possessions or family life. An ultimately more dangerous kind of secularism is intellectual, the work of those Christians who feel a special obligation to come to terms with the largely secular, and often overtly antireligious, thought of the modern world. Certainly the disorders within Catholicism which exist at the popular level would not now be so serious had it not been for the fact that for nearly two decades Catholics have been subjected to propaganda, sometimes from quasi-official church sources, which reflects un-Christian and even anti-Christian ways of thinking. (An obvious example is the uncritical assimilation of certain kinds of psychology by Christian educators and pastors.)

The changes in the Catholic church at the time of the Council and immediately afterwards produced in many people a sense of exhilaration, a feeling that the Catholic church was now getting in touch with its deepest spiritual wellsprings. Immense hopes for dramatic "renewal" were held out. These hopes in turn fed the inner spiritual restlessness already alluded to; for many, the excitement of change was itself sufficient proof that something deeply significant was going on.

Many people were satisfied in this excitement only so long as "things were happening," which meant dramatic changes in the way Catholics thought or acted. These people could not, however, endure apparent stability. The process of "renewal" was meaningful for them only so long as there were constant "breakthroughs," which most of the time meant radical departures from traditional teaching and practice. Church life was "meaningful" only insofar as somewhere on the horizon they could see the possibility of achieving certain goals which at first glance might seem unrealistic. (Thus, many reasoned in effect, if the Catholic church no longer forbids its members to eat meat on Fridays, it will eventually permit abortion and divorce.)

Soon the pace of change failed to sustain the excitement and sense of exhilaration that reformers sought. More significantly, as they quickly achieved all their professed goals of "renewal," they found themselves less and less satisfied. Gradually they were driven back to the basic question of belief itself—what they regarded as credible or incredible in the teachings of their church. Some, with at least honesty to their credit, admitted that indeed very little seemed credible, and they left the church. Many others, however, remained members, even sought for themselves positions of leadership, and strove, sometimes fanatically, to remake that church to fit their own specifications. This process continues to the present time and is at the heart of the deep divisions which wrack the Catholic church.

On one level many proponents of change in the church were woefully naive about its social and psychological effects. In theory it was possible to justify certain rapid transformations (in the forms of worship, for example, or in the discipline of religious orders), but in practice these often induced great confusion and demoralization among those exposed to them—not only to the relatively unsophisticated people in the pews but even to those, such as priests and nuns, who could be assumed to be knowledgeable about the real meaning of their faith. The effects of this confusion—more psychological and symbolic than doctrinal but having serious repercussions as to doctrine—are still being acutely felt. Often Catholics appear frozen in a kind of uncomprehending agnosticism about anything in their faith which has become "controversial." They search for formulations of that faith which will avoid the hard questions of belief and behavior.

The process of "renewal" in the Catholic church has often been subverted because of the failure to formulate clear and stable criteria of what authentic renewal might be. Such criteria do exist at the highest level, in the official statements of the Second Vatican Council itself and in the pronouncements of two popes since that time. However, largely because of the psychological confusion already alluded to, these criteria have often failed to be communicated to the rank and file of the church, including, once again, many priests and nuns.

Thus changes in what the Catholic church calls "religious life" (organized religious orders for men and women) were first proposed as ways of strengthening that life. It was freely predicted that, once nuns discarded their "medieval" styles of dress and became more "open to the world," new members would flock to join. In fact the reverse has happened. The most self-consciously "renewed" communities are dying, having lost the most members and attracting practically no new ones, even as some of the more traditional communities remain relatively stable in size and are even growing. Once this pattern became so overwhelmingly obvious as to be undeniable, however, reformers simply ceased saying that their aim was to provide their communities with new strength. Instead they began to speculate that it was precisely their historical purpose to pass away.

Similar signs took place with regard to the anomaly also noted previously—changes justified originally as returns to New Testament practice (as in worship) quickly became the pursuit of contemporary fashions. Once this shift also had become too obvious to deny, proponents of change ceased claiming the Scripture as their chief warrant and began to talk about "reading the signs of the times."

Catholic reformers have found themselves plagued by the problem which has affected liberal Protestants for over a century—determining what does or does not belong to the core of faith, what may not be sacrificed. Liberal Protestants of a century ago thought they had identified the essence of the New Testament and that they could separate it from cultural trappings which were hindrances to that faith. In reality liberals have proven to be, in each generation, quite willing to sacrifice precisely that which the previous generation thought of as central and sacrosanct. So also Catholic reformers in 1965 often took militant stands on behalf of every doctrine of the church which was officially "defined." Rapidly, however, they began to abandon the very concept of sacrosanct and defined belief, and they began to invoke merely the spirit of the age as their ultimate criterion of truth. Often this shift occurred without members of the church even being aware that it was taking place.

The unravelling of a religious tradition can sometimes occur over matters that objectively might seem peripheral. The psychological effects of abandoning the Latin liturgy in the Catholic church have been incalculable. Particularly sensitive are points of practical discipline which are not of the essence of a particular faith but which loom large in people's lives. Priestly celibacy—required as a discipline by the Catholic church but not regarded as dogmatically necessary—is an obvious example. Often Catholics who were spiritually restless first expressed that restlessness by strong public criticism of aspects of lived faith which were admittedly not essential, such as the style of dress worn by nuns. In making such criticisms they could point to their own firm distinction between matters of faith and matters of culture. However, not only did the abandonment of these peripheral elements often have devastating psychological consequences, it was also often the preliminary to attacks on matters which are necessary to faith. Within evangelicalism, it might be suggested that disputes over, for example, the consumption of alcohol could serve a similar historical function. The point is not that traditional customs must be maintained at all costs, but that church members should at least not be lulled into a false security because dissatisfaction seems to focus only on secondary issues.

In 1960 the Catholic church seemed like a fortress impregnably guarded—a steel-framed, reinforced concrete house surrounded by a series of daunting walls, along with other safety devices like flood lights and burglar alarms. It seemed plausible that some of this excess security could safely be eliminated, leaving the fortress still safe. To vary the metaphor, Catholics in general, and especially the clergy (including nuns), seemed so conservative in matters of belief that even a measure of thaw would leave them relatively solid.

But history provides many examples of the process by which, as the popular saying has it, people move from one extreme to the other, and this was precisely what happened among many Catholics. This has proven to be true even of whole nations, such as the Netherlands, where Catholicism before the Council was reputedly at its most rigid and is now the most radical. It is true now of certain religious orders, especially of women. Such groups have changed their beliefs, and indeed their whole mode of life, with unimaginable speed and thoroughness in less than twenty years.

This too holds serious warning for evangelicals tempted to take comfort in the fact that their faith is, socially, so firm—even rigid in some cases—that a measure of loosening would have no serious consequences. In fact, it is precisely the most demanding faiths—those with the best-established systems of doctrine and discipline—that invite extreme responses. A useful test of the authenticity of a religious faith is its capacity to produce embittered apostates. If it does not do so, in all likelihood it is because the church in question has not made strong demands on its members, has in fact accommodated itself to their own demands. There are no embittered refugees from liberal Protestantism, simply because liberal Protestantism fails to establish a firm identity in the souls of most of its adherents.

The point, once again, is not to argue that evangelical leaders should resist all requests for change. No ecclesiastical institution can remain purely immobile generation after generation. However, every change must at least be carefully thought out, prayed about, and implemented with the greatest concern for its possible effects on the whole body of the church.

Many well-meaning Catholics of the conciliar era (again including many priests and nuns) evinced an unrecognized kind of spiritual pride, once more connected with their ostensible desire to recover a purer faith than the one they had inherited. This pride took the form of saying, in effect, that while other people (or earlier generations) might need various kinds of social and cultural support for their faith, the gifted new generation did not. For example, the Catholic church had erected various safeguards to protect the celibacy of those vowed to that life. Now many celibates began to act as though such safeguards were unnecessary, that their own heroic virtue and good sense would be enough to sustain them in their commitments. Quickly, however, as the safeguards were discarded, the commitment itself became harder and harder to sustain.

Once again, this has been on a deeper level than mere discipline. Many intellectual Catholics of a quarter century ago complained of living in a religious ghetto, in which the plausibility of even the most basic Catholic beliefs was sustained in part by the fact that many other people shared those same beliefs and by the fact that institutions, such as social clubs and communications media, had been set up precisely for that purpose. However, once reformers set about dismantling or abandoning those institutions, they discovered, often enough, that their faith was indeed lost. Ironically, while they often patronizingly assumed that only the simple needed such social supports, the simple in many instances have turned out to be faithful even despite the collapse of social supports, while it has been precisely the proponents of a purer faith who found belatedly that they needed them.

No understanding of the unravelling of American Catholicism in the past twenty years is possible without paying attention to the fact of Catholic social assimilation. The studies of Father Andrew Greeley[2], among others, seem to show that Catholics had indeed begun to arrive in the mainstream of American life by the early 1960s, judging from income, education, and other indices.

This sense of "arrival" coincided with the Second Vatican Council and also coincided with the election of the country's first Catholic president. For many, John F. Kennedy symbolized the success of American Catholics, not only in the sense of their having at last attained the nation's highest office but also in the sense that supposedly all hostility to their faith had now been overcome.

The latter fond belief was dubious. What rather happened was that much of the traditional anti-Catholic hostility which had directly Protestant roots had evaporated, to be replaced immediately by a wider kind of hostility originating from mainly secular sources, a hostility which is directed at all genuine religion and tends to focus on the Catholic church as simply the most visible target.

Virtually everyone who has studied President Kennedy's life has concluded that his religion meant little to him. He was not well-schooled in his faith, nor very devout. Privately, he is reported to have favored legalized abortion, even before it had become a major political issue. In fact, once elected, Kennedy proceeded to show in every way possible that his faith did not seriously inform or govern his political behavior. It could, in fact, be said that this demonstration was the very price he paid for disarming his critics, and that he set a pattern that has been followed by numerous Catholic politicians since that time. Today's litmus test of a docile Catholic politician is the willingness to support legalized abortion, and many Catholic politicians—Senator Edward Kennedy, Speaker of the House "Tip" O'Neill, Governor Mario Cuomo, former Congresswoman Geraldine Ferraro, and even the former Jesuit Congressman Robert Drinan—have passed that test.

The twin facts of their own "arrival" in the mainstream of American life and the election of one of their own to the presidency also affected many Catholics' understanding of the inner meaning of their faith. Ecumenism, which was encouraged by the Second Vatican Council, was misunderstood to mean a kind of doctrinal indifference, with ecumenical relations based mainly on good will (or, in some cases, on a shared disenchantment with the traditions of all the churches).

But the wider "ecumenism" towards secular society was even more deadly. For many Catholics chose to believe, by the mid-1960s, that not only was the culture around them not hostile to their faith, there was little in that faith which made them different from Protestants or even from non-believers. They chose to believe that an age of amorphous good will had descended on the land, in which religious differences had proven to be illusory.

There are, of course, broad areas where Christians can meaningfully cooperate with non-believers in the continuing life of society. However, many Catholics were left first surprised, then nonplussed, and finally silenced when a major assault on their beliefs—the legalization of abortion—confronted them ten years after President Kennedy's death. Although the fight against abortion has galvanized many Catholics into a new awareness of how the surrounding culture does threaten their faith, and to a new militancy about it, many others have sunk into a permanent stance of indifference, evasion, or supine surrender before the world's demands. Little by little they alter their beliefs, especially on sensitive issues like sexual behavior, to conform to what "enlightened" secular opinion requires.

Arguably, evangelicals have only fairly recently achieved the level of social acceptance and success that Catholics, as a group, achieved around 1960. Arguably, therefore, such a sense of "arrival" might have similar deleterious consequences on the solidity of their own faith. There is a political parallel in President Jimmy Carter, who, although probably more devout than John Kennedy was, nevertheless used the authority of his office in many ways to promote secular values, as in his sponsorship of the White House Conference on Families in 1980. There is no doubt that the abortion issue makes many evangelicals uncomfortable, especially those with public positions to protect. Many evangelicals, like many Catholics, are not comfortable taking stands that the secular world brands as backward and sectarian.

The worst lies are those told to oneself, and in order for Christians to become entirely comfortable with the secular culture they must eventually tell themselves many lies. Ultimately, their faith becomes systematically redefined not only to meet direct assaults but even in an attempt to anticipate and disarm such attacks. Liberal Protestantism has for 150 years constantly looked over its shoulder at its "cultured despisers" and has taken the secular intellectual community as the primary constituency whom it must impress. Catholics began doing the same thing a quarter century ago, and it may now be the evangelicals' turn.

The role of the secular media in all this can scarcely be exaggerated. Arguably, the troubles of modern Catholicism began when discontented elements within the church joined with strategically placed individuals in the media, in effect, to hijack the Second Vatican Council even before it was over. The great majority of Catholics who never had an opportunity to make a careful study of the Council were told, through the media, that it represented in effect the Catholic church's coming to terms with the modern world, its admission of all its past errors, which it was now repudiating. Given this version of the Council, it is little wonder that many Catholics are now suspicious of anything the church teaches. They have been told that all of its doctrines are subject to radical revision under the pressure of time.

On one level the media simply have a fascination with change and conflict and thus tend to exaggerate conflictual elements in contemporary religious life. However, the media are also dominated by people who are religious sceptics and outright secularists. Personally, they have little sympathy for any kind of orthodox Christianity, and they instinctively sympathize with every element in every church which promises radical changes in that church, which is willing publicly to denounce the church for its "backward," "rigid," "inhumane" teachings and practices.

Discontented elements in the churches soon learn how to make use of the media for their own purposes. The attention the media is willing to bestow on them gives them an importance, and an apparent strength, far beyond their numbers. Most important, the fact that they garner largely favorable publicity means that many otherwise contented church members begin to gravitate towards the dissenters, simply because dissent appears to be in the inevitable wave of the future. Many church members did not realize that their church was "oppressive" and "backward" until they were told so by the media.

Such a situation skews church life to an extraordinary degree and constitutes an enormous temptation even to relatively "moderate" people to tailor their view of religion to the categories which the media find interesting. In concentrated form the media represent the stark pressure of unbelief brought to bear on contemporary Christianity.

Higher education has an ultimately even more important effect, since the universities have for a long time been the ultimate arbiters of intellectual respectability in the Western world. Prior to the 1960s, Catholic universities thought of themselves as conscious alternatives to secular institutions, and to some extent in an antagonistic relationship with them.

Catholic schools claimed that their teaching of philosophy and theology, to say nothing of the religious influence on other disciplines, provided their students with a better and deeper education than they could obtain on more prestigious secular campuses.

Beginning about 1965, however, Catholic universities have simply rushed to emulate the secular schools as much as possible. Most of them still find a place for Catholic theology and philosophy, but dissent from official Catholic church teaching is now more often the norm than the exception. A governing myth of contemporary Catholic colleges is that they represent the thoughtful, forward-looking element of the church which is emancipating itself from the narrowness of the past and the obscurantism of official Catholic church leaders. Much of the task of the Catholic colleges now is to assimilate their students as much as possible into a secular worldview, with a smattering of liberal theology as a garnish. Even where there are blatant conflicts between Catholic doctrine and secular academic wisdom (as in certain kinds of psychology), little notice is taken of that fact.

Most broadly, Catholic intellectuals, with some exceptions, do not think of themselves as possessed of a legitimate worldview which is different from, and to some extent in conflict with, that of unbelievers. They do not see their intellectual task as that of high-level evangelization of unbelievers so much as that of "evangelizing" the church with the best of secular wisdom.

Those familiar with the situation of the evangelical colleges and seminaries will themselves have to assess whether such a pattern is emerging in those places. Given the present social and cultural situation of evangelicalism, it is not unlikely that it is.

As alluded to several times, sexual belief and behavior is one of the most sensitive points of tension between orthodox Christianity on the one hand and liberal religion and secular culture on the other. Christian attitudes towards sex are therefore an excellent index to the health of the churches.

Sexual morality has been bitterly debated within Roman Catholicism for twenty years, and there are organized groups striving to undermine traditional teaching at almost every point. In this respect the situation of evangelicalism is not wholly reassuring. The embarrassment many evangelicals seem to feel over the abortion issue is one example. So also are evangelical treatises which address questions of sexual morality, such as Lewis Smedes's *Sex for Christians* and *Mere Morality* and—more blatant—Letha Scamzoni's and Virginia Ramey Mollenkott's *Is the Homosexual My Neighbor?*

Politics has proven to be both a divisive and a necessary activity of contemporary Christians, necessary because there often are crucial moral issues raised in a political context, divisive because there are diametrically opposite views on what the churches' role in politics ought to be.

The evangelical left wing centered on *Sojourners* magazine has attracted a great deal of attention and is (along with other, less extreme examples) pointed to as showing how evangelicalism, long stereotyped as apolitical or politically conservative, is changing.

It is worth noting, from the Catholic experience, that leftist politics has been one of the most important means by which discontented Catholics have "liberated" themselves from their faith. Although there have been doctrinally orthodox Catholic leftists, like the late Dorothy Day of the Catholic Worker movement, most Catholic leftists, even if they began by invoking unimpeachably orthodox theological arguments on behalf of their commitments, have ended by embracing a secular and even sometimes anti-Christian ideology. The so-called liberation theologians of Latin America are a major example. Thousands of Catholics in the pew, however, traversed the route from orthodox belief to complete secularization after Vatican II through the medium of political involvement. (Often the political commitment was itself abandoned after the individual had first used it to shuck off the religious identity.) A favorite argument of the 1960s was that a religious reason for political activity was superfluous—the social need was itself sufficient as a motive.

*Sojourners* represents an ambiguous phenomenon. Some of its positions, such as its seemingly blind devotion to the Sandinista government of Nicaragua, suggest sheer political ideology. Its response to other kinds of controversial questions, such as feminism, suggests that, contrary to its claims, it does not draw primary inspiration from the teachings of Christianity but from trendy secular sources.

Of course, the gospel cannot be made captive to right-wing politics any more than to left-wing, and legitimate criticism can and must be made of religious groups which blindly endorse every right-wing agenda. However, such groups—those loosely called the Religious Right—are still largely marginalized in American life, treated by respectable opinion as bizarre and of dubious sanity. To be an outspoken Moral Majoritarian, in most American communities, is to risk obloquy and ostracism. Evangelicals who espouse left-wing positions, on the other hand, can expect to be praised and even lionized in the media and on college campuses. In effect, like many Catholics before them, they are told, "You are a *good* kind of evangelical, not one of those bad kinds like Jerry Falwell." The urge to demonstrate, at every opportunity, that they are indeed not like Jerry Falwell is one which evangelicals ought to resist. They may indeed feel a gulf between themselves and the Moral Majority, but it is fatal to allow identity to be defined so negatively, and especially to allow it to be defined by those who have no sympathy for the evangelical position.

The exercise of discipline by the authorities within a particular denomination is crucial to whether or not the denomination begins to suffer serious internal crisis. Even relatively conservative modern Christians are likely to be uncomfortable at the thought of using firm discipline against a fellow Christian. However, failure to exercise authority, where matters of faith are at stake, is ultimately the worst kind of uncharity and can have devastating consequences for the whole church.

Many Catholic bishops, in the period after 1965, seem to have made the decision that they would not exercise such discipline. Perhaps too much has been made of the proclamation of Gamaliel in Acts of the Apostles, when he suggested that the Sanhedrin simply wait to see whether the new religious phenomenon was actually from the Spirit. Often, by the time it becomes clear that a certain phenomenon is not, grave damage has been done to the faith of many people.

The exercise of authority by those given that authority is more than disciplinary. It is also, perhaps even more importantly, symbolic. If church members see the teachings and practices of their church continually questioned and even denied publicly by people who hold some position of responsibility—seminary professors, for example, or directors of religious education—they naturally conclude that the teachings and practices themselves are in doubt. Otherwise, they reason, church authorities would move to reaffirm them and to stem the attack.

The modernist drive against religious doctrine will not finally wear itself out. It is not satiated by lesser victories. Eventually, if not checked, it will assault even the deepest of Christian beliefs, since it aims at nothing less than calling all things into doubt. Only vigorous teaching and discipline by church leaders can prevent this from happening.

# Notes

1. James Hitchcock, *The Decline and Fall of Radical Catholicism* (New York: Herder and Herder, 1971).
2. See, for example, his *The American Catholic, a Social Portrait* (New York: Basic Books, 1977).

# FOUR

# Christian Faith and Twentieth-Century Ideologies

*Donald G. Bloesch*

*The Ideological Spell*

L IKE THE FALSE PROPHETS IN ANCIENT ISRAEL, today's self-styled prophets are giving misleading counsel to both church and state.

On the one hand, we find those who hail the Sandinistas as the shining hope of Latin America, and the Contras as political criminals allied with the discredited Somoza regime. On the other, we hear those who label the Sandinistas as agents of an international Communist conspiracy, and portray the Contras as freedom fighters comparable to the early American revolutionaries.

Again, there are those who urge support for the sanctuary movement in which churches open their doors to illegal refugees from Central American regimes listed by our State Department as friendly states, such as El Salvador and Guatemala. On the opposite side are those who accuse the sanctuary movement of being duped by left-wing propaganda designed to embarrass the Reagan administration. Such persons seem oblivious to the right-wing death squads in various Central American nations that have been given virtually free reign to silence all dissent.

On the subject of peace, we are also bombarded by discordant voices. The Ban the Bomb movement calmly assures us that peace can become a reality by the virtual unilateral dismantling of our nuclear arsenal. The Peace through Strength movement calls for shoring up our nuclear defense as the only way to maintain the balance of power in a precarious world. Both sides see human ingenuity and diligence as the key to peace.

In the area of economics, we find those who contend that economic prosperity lies in the unfettered market and that economic ruin has its source in unwarranted interference by big government in the private sector. Poverty is traced to indolence and apathy, rather than to exploitation by corporations. Their opponents argue that only by state regulation of the means of production can justice be ensured for all classes in society.

While there is some truth in all these voices, they also betray a narrowing of vision that accounts for their often naive and simplistic solutions to social and political problems. The confusion in their counsel derives from what I call the ideological spell, the blurring of one's perceptions by an uncritical identification with a particular social cause. An ideology paints the world in black and white and allows for no greys. It therefore loses sight of the ambiguous and uncertain character of all human enterprises.

Christian faith can ill afford to align itself with any ideology lest it lose its anchor in the transcendent. When we hear that the "evil empire" is the Soviet Union, for example, we as Christians must remind world leaders that the ultimate evil empire exists within all of us, that it cuts through both West and East, right and left. I am not suggesting that Christians can remain aloof from the social struggle and must refrain from making relative judgments concerning the right and wrong in any social conflict. My point is that in their judgments they must keep in mind that all human endeavor lies under the divine judgment, that before God no one's hands are clean.

## *Faith and Ideology*

Surely one of the most pressing issues in theology today is the enigmatic relation between faith and ideology. Does faith in the living God revealed in Jesus Christ need an ideological framework in order to relate to the practical issues of the time? Should faith enter into an alliance with an ideology in order to maintain its relevance? Can the truth of faith be brought into the service of a strategic goal without losing its redemptive impact and power?

The concept of "ideology" has a long history in Western civilization, but ever since Marx and Engels it has come to represent a false consciousness that distorts the realities of the cultural and religious situation. It connotes a bias rooted in cultural and economic factors that prevents people from seeing the whole of reality.

An ideology might be defined as an orientation toward life and the world that serves to advance the interests of a particular class or group in society. While its focus is on social-empirical reality, the workaday life in the world, it colors one's understanding of every aspect of life. It generally arises as a protest against some social wrong or as a reaction to some perceived threat to social order.

An ideology is invariably reductionistic. By giving simplistic answers to difficult problems, it hides or ignores the complexity and ambiguity of the situation. It therefore constricts rather than broadens one's social vision.

Whereas pure philosophy is engaged in the dispassionate pursuit of truth, ideology connotes an attempt to bend truth to practical ends. By contrast, theology places the emphasis on obedience to the truth.

Characteristic of all ideology is its reliance on propaganda rather than dialogue to achieve its goals. While it may give lip service to an open investigation of the facts, the results are already predetermined. An ideology serves to disguise "real abuses and replaces rational arguments by an appeal to emotion."[1]

Ideologies in effect function as substitute salvations, since the knowledge they purport to give is redemptive insofar as it provides "existential hope and guidance."[2] An ideology is also inclined to be totalistic in that its claims penetrate every area of human existence, and it can tolerate no alternative view of reality.

Reinhold Niebuhr is one theologian who has been ready to acknowledge the ideological taint in human reasoning. He maintains that no religion or political system is exempt from this taint; even the vision of those who champion the rights of the oppressed is vulnerable to ideological distortion. The task of theology is to recognize the ideological temptation and always to struggle against it.

This is certainly not the prevailing position on the current theological scene. Liberation theologian Juan Luis Segundo believes ideology to be salutary and necessary, since every religious community needs a conceptual system that organizes and directs practical human life.[3] An ideology becomes stifling and oppressive only when it is divorced from a transcendent religious faith. Elisabeth Schüssler-Fiorenza concludes that theology will always serve certain interests, and therefore it "has to reflect and critically evaluate its primary motives and allegiance." If it is to be on the side of the poor and oppressed, it has "to abandon its so-called objectivity and . . . become partisan."[4]

My position is closer to Niebuhr's. I see a fundamental contradiction rather than a congruity between ideology and faith. Whereas faith calls for the criticism of reality in the light of eternity, ideology critiques reality on the basis of a social theory. Faith questions all human presuppositions and assumptions;[5] ideology demands a blind adherence to particular assumptions about man and society. Faith seeks understanding and reconciliation between opposing parties in society; ideology tries to crush all those who stand in the way of human progress. Faith is an opening of one's inward eyes to the action of God in history that brings an end to the existing world order; ideology is a vision of the triumph of human ingenuity in building a new world. Faith recognizes that truth can make its own way in the world; ideology sees the efficacy of truth dependent on human strategy and technique. Faith is content to wait for the full disclosure of truth; an ideology claims a premature possession of truth. Faith makes use of ideas as aids in understanding the mystery of God's self-revelation in Christ; an ideology regards ideas as tools in social engineering. Faith's concern is the regeneration of the human spirit; the overriding concern in ideology is the restructuring of society.

Segundo is right that every ideology has a religious or metaphysical basis. Yet upon close examination this most often proves to be a religion rooted in cultural aspirations and is therefore to be contrasted with the faith that comes to us by revelation. Both faith and religion are generally dismissed as obstacles to human liberation by ideologies of the left, since they turn people's attention away from the agonizing issues of this world to some other world. Ideologies of the right, on the other hand, are usually very open to religion, which they see as buttressing the interests of the classes in power. From this perspective, religion is valued for its social utility but not for its truth. Religion becomes a sacred canopy that legitimates "human social arrangements by projecting them as our sacred and cosmic frame of reference."[6]

In our day, ideologies are coming more and more to reflect tribalistic loyalties rather than class interests *per se*. When people give their ultimate allegiance not to class but to race, nation, or ethnic heritage, then an ideology takes on an entirely different complexion. Its basis is no longer the hope of economic betterment but the vision of ethnocentric unity and identity. We see this new thrust in ideology in pan-Arabism, Polish nationalism, Russian hegemonism, Zionism, black African tribalism, Christian Nationalism in South Africa and communalism in India. I believe that class interests will always be present to some degree in any ideology, but the stirrings of racial or national consciousness may be far more significant in our time.

One should keep in mind that not all people associated with a particular ideological camp are ideologues. That is to say, there are undoubtedly many who have only a tangential relationship to an ideology and are therefore not fully committed to its social program. Others may once have been under the spell of an ideology but are now breaking away through disillusionment with its promises. An idealogue, by contrast, is totally committed to an ideological vision and therefore impervious to the persuasive power of reason. Not all card-carrying Communists, for example, are hard-nosed ideological Marxists, nor are all feminists committed unreservedly to the goals of feminism as an ideology. It is important to make such distinctions if we are successfully to combat ideology in the present age.

## Types of Ideology

Among the ideologies competing to be king of the hill in our time, perhaps none is producing more dismay in the academic establishment than conservatism. This train of thought, which by all accounts has made dramatic strides in recent years, vigorously upholds free enterprise, regional autonomy, and rugged individualism. The entrepreneur takes the place of the saint as the model of the "new man." The laws of the marketplace are practically equated with the laws of God.

Conservatism in its American form has its sources in classical liberalism, Social Darwinism, and Transcendentalism. Among its luminaries are Adam Smith, David Ricardo,

Charles de Montesquieu, Edmund Burke, Thomas Jefferson, John Locke, Ralph Waldo Emerson, and Herbert Spencer. In our day it is defended in varying degrees by such provocative and scintillating writers as Russell Kirk, George Gilder, Ayn Rand, Irving Kristol, Patrick Buchanan, Michael Novak, William Safire, and William Buckley. Emerson voiced the credo of this ideology when he asserted: "Wealth brings with it its own checks and balances. The basis of political economy is non-interference. The only safe rule is found in the self-adjusting meter of demand and supply. Do not legislate."[7]

In this orientation, bourgeois acquisitiveness is generally applauded, indicating as it does the desire to better one's condition by diligent application. The happy outcome will be "the improvement of *everyone's* condition."[8] According to Adam Smith, the laws of supply and demand will inevitably lead "to the greatest number and quality of goods at the lowest price for the greatest number of people."[9]

Ideological conservatives give primacy to economic freedom, believing that this will result in a world where material wants and needs are satisfied to the highest degree possible. The liberation that they eulogize is freedom from governmental control and regulation. The principal sinners are the big spenders. Poverty stems from slothfulness and limited social horizon rather than the exploitation and oppression of workers by big corporations. Among the enemies that need to be combated, none are so sinister as the misguided idealists who, in the name of social equality, try to impose a system of progressive taxation upon the public so that the industrious are penalized for the sake of those who will not pull their own weight.

Though ideological conservatism embraces the economic system of free enterprise capitalism, the latter must not be confused with the former. An economic theory as such is not an ideology, but it may lend itself for use by an ideology, which is inspired by a mythological version of a perfect society or new social order.

While the consistent conservatives seek not only economic but also religious and political freedom, a number of conservatives associated with the new populism call for government regulation of private morality. One can detect growing tensions between those who decry governmental intervention in all areas of life and those who favor it in the area of morals.

In opposition to classical liberalism, now called conservatism, there has arisen, especially since the Depression years, the ideology of welfare liberalism. While continuing to affirm faith in human progress and perceiving the hope of the human race in primarily economic terms, it calls for state regulation of the means of production to overcome the disparity between rich and poor. It does not wish to stifle human initiative, but it sees the public good as taking precedence over individual prosperity. The social planner is more highly regarded than the entrepreneur. The benevolent government takes the place of the unfettered market as the source of human well-being. The orientation of welfare liberalism is collectivist and statist. Justice and equality have priority over economic freedom.

Welfare liberalism draws its support not only from disinherited minorities and the working class but also from what Peter Berger and Richard Neuhaus call the "new class." These are the people who favor increased governmental intervention in all aspects of society. Their aim is to create a new kind of individual—one who is other-directed rather than inner-directed, who is sensitive to the needs of those less fortunate in society. A great many of these people, who have upward mobility on the economic scale, are employed in the rapidly growing public sector of society and are therefore dependent on government aid for their livelihood. They generally belong to the teaching and service professions as opposed to the business and farming interests which are likely to throw their support to ideological conservatism. Neuhaus aptly calls them a "new elite," since they "make a living by minting and marketing the metaphors by which they think society should be ordered."[10] Whereas the bourgeois values of the old elite were based on the production and distribution of material goods, "the new class produces and distributes symbolic goods—knowledge and enlightenment."[11]

Welfare liberalism might be considered a transitional stage between conservatism and socialism. Both welfare liberalism and socialism in its modern phase are to be seen as reacting to the supposed inequities spawned by capitalism.

It is socialism that has given the modern world the captivating vision of a classless society where all inequity and exploitation are eradicated. Socialism advocates state ownership of the means of production and state control of the means of distribution for the sake of the welfare of the masses. Corporations, which allegedly create and exploit the poor, need to be abolished if social justice is to become a tangible reality. Protesting against the concentration of wealth in the hands of a few (as in capitalism), it favors the distribution of wealth to the whole populace.

Socialism has its intellectual roots in the writings of Jean Jacques Rousseau, Karl Marx, Friedrich Engels, Louis Blanc, Ferdinand Lassalle, Eduard Bernstein, Leon Trotsky and V.I. Lenin. The most consistent type of socialism is Marxist-Leninism, which upholds a proletarian dictatorship as the necessary means for an equitable distribution of goods in society. Socialism has also taken democratic forms, for example, in the British Labor Party and the socialist parties of France, Germany, the United States, and Scandinavia. As in the case of classical liberalism, socialism has been embraced by a significant number of Christian theologians, among them Paul Tillich, Frederick Denison Maurice, Leonhard Ragaz, Friedrich-Wilhelm Marquardt, and the early Reinhold Niebuhr.

Socialism seeks the breakup of hierarchy and the leveling of authority. It champions free medical aid and universal education. Yet it places its faith in a socially enlightened elite of welfare planners who may be democratically elected or who may be compelled to seize power by military force. The socialist state is collectivist, but its purported aim is not the extension of power as an end in itself but power in the service of justice. Its purpose is the amelioration of the misery of the masses for whom it speaks.

By its very nature, socialism is utopian, since it envisages a social order free from strife and exploitation, one that can be ushered in by legislation, even by violent revolution. Socialism can be criticized for its unwavering and unsubstantiated faith in the innate goodness of humanity and its blindness to the corrupting influence of centralized power. Like both classical and welfare liberalism, socialism is an Enlightenment creed: its hope is in the infinite possibilities resident in the human soul rather than in a divine promise to redeem humankind from its iniquity. It presupposes a belief in human perfectibility and inevitable human progress, both of which patently conflict with the biblical understanding of the inevitability of tragedy in human history because of human sin.

Harboring many of the same utopian illusions is feminism, which also divides humankind between the oppressed and the oppressors. It is best understood as an ideology for the liberation of women from oppression and exploitation by a sexist and patriarchal society. The adversary in feminism is not monopolistic corporations nor the industrial-military complex (though these generally remain objects of stricture) but the patriarchal life and worldview that presumably holds women in a subordinate or inferior position. Feminists loudly complain that women are the most oppressed of all segments of society, since they are systematically kept from the reins of power. Like socialists, feminists are intent on breaking up hierarchy in social relationships. With socialists and welfare liberals, they zealously throw their support behind affirmative action legislation designed to ensure for minorities equal opportunity in job selection and an equal voice in business decisions.

Feminists are inclined to see the traditional family as a prime obstacle to women's liberation. In place of the traditional family where the man is considered the sole head and breadwinner, feminists promote the egalitarian family where decisions are mutually agreed upon and where each party is free to pursue his or her own career.

Authority is rooted in the experience of women who have been made aware of their status as oppressed persons in a male-dominated world. Men who can empathize with this experience are welcomed as comrades in the quest for a more just society. Feminists are inspired by the vision of a holistic humanity where men and women work together in harmony as equals.

In order to achieve their ends, feminists advocate consciousness-raising—the art of cultivating sensitivity to the needs and plight of the oppressed. Consciousness-raising must take place in public education, and this is why feminists are so intent on rewriting texts to make sure that women's history is not neglected and that inclusive language is always used.

One cannot properly understand feminism without some comprehension of its adversary—patriarchalism. Patriarchalism is the ideology that legitimates patriarchy, the rule of man over women and children. It is both an ancient and a modern ideology and is by no means monolithic. In its classical form, it holds that man is the sole head of the family as well as its provider and protector. Human relationships are understood in terms of hierarchy in which the headship of man in the family is analogous to the lordship of kings and feudal barons. The main role of woman is to bear and raise children and to comfort and satisfy her husband. According to Aristotle, "ruling-class Greek males are the natural exemplars of mind or reason, while women, slaves, and barbarians are the naturally servile people, represented by the body and passions, which must be ruled by the 'head.'"[12] Women and children are the property of the husband and father and therefore have no rights of their own. In medieval civilization, classical patriarchy was humanized to a degree, but the male was still regarded as the norm of humanity. Indeed, it was commonly held that only man is created directly in the image of God and that woman participates in this image only by being joined to man. Patriarchalism was also evident in Reformation Protestantism, which valued women chiefly for their capability of bearing male heirs and thereby ensuring the perpetuation of property and the family name. Both Calvin and Luther transcended this mentality at times, but they nevertheless still thought in hierarchical and dualistic terms when describing human relationships. Patriarchalism was more successfully challenged in Puritanism, Pietism, and Quakerism, where the woman was depicted as a partner in ministry and the door was opened for women to assume positions of spiritual leadership.

It is interesting to ascertain how ideology colors one's understanding of basic Christian truths. In patriarchalism, God is the kingly Lord who arbitrarily elects some to salvation and others to damnation. In feminism, God is the creative force within us that enables us to realize our human potential. For patriarchalism, sin is rebellion against authority, thereby preparing the way for anarchy. For feminism, sin is the exploitation of the poor and powerless and acquiescence to this exploitation. Whereas patriarchalism sees the chief sin as pride, feminism views the principal sin as passive resignation to social evil. In patriarchalism, salvation lies in childlike faith in an almighty Father. In feminism, salvation is to be found in the rediscovery of authentic humanity and in assertiveness in the cause of equality.

This ideological polarity becomes especially evident in the current abortion controversy. Because feminism upholds female autonomy, it naturally supports the free choice position on abortion. Because patriarchalism accentuates the reproductive role of women, it generally supports the right to life position.

One ideology that belongs peculiarly to the twentieth century is fascism. Fascism draws upon various intellectual sources including neo-idealism, vitalism, activism, and the cult of the hero. It was profoundly influenced by such philosophical luminaries as Nietzsche, Carlyle, Pareto, Sorel, and Herbert Spencer, the philosopher of Social Darwinism. While classical liberalism stresses property rights, and modern welfare liberalism and socialism focus on human rights, fascism's emphasis is on national rights. While modern liberalism celebrates diversity and pluralism, fascism seeks a state that is racially and ethnically homogeneous. Whereas welfare liberalism and socialism are committed to social planning, fascism protests against creeping bureaucracy and rational controls. Although it advocates a strong centralized state, it sees this state personified in a charismatic leader who becomes a father figure to the masses. Ideally it seeks an alliance of government with big business and big labor in a corporate state for the purpose of creating a homogeneous national unit.

While a fascist state is authoritarian, what differentiates it from a military dictatorship is its ability to provide an ideology that gives people a sense of national destiny, an incentive to perform feats of often heroic proportions. In a system that places national honor and security above all else, the main enemies are minorities that are unwilling or unable to assimilate. But threats from abroad are by no means ignored. In foreign policy fascism is likely to be adventurist and expansionist, for it recognizes that national and racial survival are contingent on taking the offensive against unfriendly states and peoples.

Unlike classical liberalism, welfare liberalism, and socialism, all of which have their roots in the Enlightenment, fascism draws from the age of Romanticism, which celebrates the irrational and the heroic. Violence is seen as more efficacious than rational persuasion, even as redemptive. Fascism triumphed in Nazi Germany and in Italy under Mussolini, but fascist ideas have also found a lodging in Spain under the Falangists, in Argentina under the Peronists, and in South Africa, under the Christian Nationalists.

Because of our democratic heritage with its tolerance of divergent opinions and life-styles, fascism would seem to have little hope of success in America. Yet if our country should ever sink into a severe depression with inflation and unemployment out of hand, and if racial and ethnic minorities at the same time became more vocal in the demand for full equality, I could conceive of a situation in which people might turn to a charismatic figure who would promise social and national security at the price of giving up elemental freedoms. An upsurge in xenophobia could create a climate of receptivity to a fascist scenario. The American brand of fascism might well give eloquent praise to the ideals and values associated with democracy and capitalism, but in actuality it would crush these ideals in the attempt to forge a national consensus.

Just as socialism and welfare liberalism have a certain affinity with feminism, uniting in their call for federal laws against discrimination and supportive of affirmative action, so fascism appears to be congruous with patriarchalism. But appearances can be deceptive. Even though in its rhetoric it defends traditional family values, in practice it subordinates the family to the all-powerful state. Its opposition to abortion is rooted not in a respect for life but in a desire to perpetuate the *Volk* or people on which the national security state rests.

One final ideology should be mentioned: technological liberalism, in which both property rights and human rights are subordinated to technological growth. We need to recognize that pragmatists and technocrats can be just as ideological as new rightists and leftists. The vision of a technological practopia is the emerging ideology of the center, and it could be argued that that vision is slowly but surely replacing both the traditional, patriarchal ideal of a stratified society and the Marxist ideal of a classless society. It may well signify a partial synthesis of the opportunity state of classical liberalism and the welfare state of modern liberalism. We should pay serious attention to Pope John Paul II's condemnation of an "ideology of technology," which imposes "the primacy of matter over spirit, of things over the human person, of the technical over the moral."[13]

Still other ideologies could be included in this discussion: scientific positivism, monarchism, anarchism, pacifism, gay liberationism, syndicalism, etc. Several of these represent branches of the "metaideology"—secular humanism. We should bear in mind that ostensibly religious movements like fundamentalism, evangelicalism, and Catholicism can also become ideologies if their aim is to perpetuate a cultural ethos rather than bring a divine Word of hope and judgment to a despairing humanity.

## Ideology and Mythology

Behind every ideology is a mythology, an imaginative projection of human hopes and aspirations on the plane of history. A mythology connotes a vision of reality set forth in primal symbols that give meaning and purpose to human existence. Such a vision is rooted in a cultural faith that is invariably idolatrous, for it means enthroning cultural values and ideals.

Adam Smith's perception of reality is less empirical than mythological. Nature is personified as a beneficent force that makes use of impersonal mechanisms and laws. This "Invisible Hand," as Smith called it, should not be interfered with by governmental authority. God becomes the "Conductor of the Universe" and the "great Physician of Nature." Smith's ideology is rooted in the Enlightenment myth of pre-established harmony. It was naively believed that the free interplay of egoisms will effect a harmony or congruity between competing interests that will redound to the good of the human race as a whole.

Similarly, the so-called scientific materialism of Karl Marx proves to be based on a mythopoetic vision of reality that can be accepted only by faith, since it lacks sufficient empirical corroboration. Marx envisaged a kingdom of freedom that would signalize the liberation of the impoverished masses from the tedium of producing the bare minimum necessary for survival. He perceived human history evolving according to a materialistic dialectic from feudalism to capitalism to communism. This proletarian utopia or classless society is the mythical construct that has given Marxists the motivation to struggle against the moneyed classes in power, sometimes against almost insuperable odds. History is interpreted in the light of the class struggle, but the working class will inevitably triumph because this triumph is ordained by history itself. Marxism is actually a secularized form of post-millennialism, since the millennial promises of peace and brotherhood are to be fulfilled within history.

National Socialism was also motivated by a myth—the eternal creative power working within nature and history that drives peoples of various origins to unity and identity with their own kind. Every race, it was said, has its soul and every soul its race. The cardinal sin was mongrelization—the mixing of superior and inferior races. History was seen in terms of an ongoing conflict between "good blood," representing creativity and light, and "bad blood," the symbol of parasitism and darkness. The Teutonic destiny was the triumph of the soul of the Germanic race over inferior peoples, a triumph that is not the automatic result of evolution but the prize of heroic effort. Thus the hope of Germany was held to rest upon the realization of folkic consciousness, which would solidify the recovery of national unity and purpose. The vision of the Third Reich corresponds to the third age of the Spiritual Franciscan Joachim of Floris (d. 1202) in which peace and harmony will be restored to the nations. Joachim's influence is also conspicuous in Karl Marx's dialectic of history.

Even the modern technological state has its myth: the "Third Wave"—the practopia of the electronic-computer society, which is now being ushered in by the communications revolution. Just as the industrial state supplanted the agricultural state, so it in turn will be superseded by the computer state (reminiscent again of Joachim's three stages of history). The distribution of knowledge will characterize the new age just as the production and distribution of material goods marked the industrial age. Bureaucracy will give way to ad-hocracy, the fast-moving kinetic organization of the future. The deadening uniformity of the industrial age will be replaced by diversity and opportunity. The spirit of the entrepreneur will be reborn as corporations encourage indi-vidual initiative. Participatory democracy will supplant repre-sentative democracy. The associative man will take the place of the organization man; the former participates in managerial decisions even at the highest level rather than simply carrying out decisions made by an industrial-managerial elite. The principal struggle today is between the progressive forces representing the Third Wave and the conservative and reac-tionary forces represented by the Second Wave, and this struggle overshadows class and racial conflicts in our time. An emphasis on free will contrasts the Third Wave mythology with the historical determinism of dialectical materialism.

At the risk of oversimplification, one could say that the underlying myth that has shaped the ideologies of Western society is evolution, which here encompasses not simply biological but moral and spiritual evolution. Progress toward a yet unrealized paradise on earth becomes an irreversible principle in human history. This is the myth that inspired the Enlightenment, and it persists today—in classical liberalism or conservatism, welfare liberalism, socialism, fascism, femin-ism, and the new technological liberalism.

The primordial myth that has shaped the Orient is reincar-nation. This is the myth behind Hindu communalism, which accounts for the caste stratification in India and Nepal and explains why the accent is placed on resignation to Fate rather than revolution against the oppressor classes (as in Marxism). The myth of reincarnation also dominates in Buddhist coun-tries where the ideal is not social transformation but equanimity attained through detachment from the discords and sufferings of life.

It is important to recognize that ideologies are not equal. Some are closer to Judeo-Christian values than others, although they all contain thrusts that contravene a transcendent religious faith. Most of us would agree with Reinhold Niebuhr that the idolatry of democratic liberalism is far less noxious than the idolatries of modern secular totalitarianism, which have subjugated large parts of Europe and the Third World.[14] At the same time, we need to take seriously Barth's warning that ideologies that seem congruous with the Christian outlook on life and the world are more seductive to earnest Christians and are therefore more of a threat to the integrity of the Christian faith.

# Notes

1. Hans Küng, *Does God Exist?*, trans. Edward Quinn (New York: Doubleday, 1980), p. 124.
2. Peter L. Berger and Hansfried Kellner, *Sociology Reinterpreted* (New York: Doubleday Anchor Books, 1981), p. 144.
3. Juan Luis Segundo, *Faith and Ideologies*, trans. John Drury (Maryknoll, NY: Orbis Books, 1984).
4. Elisabeth Schüssler-Fiorenza, "Feminist Theology as a Critical Theology of Liberation" in Walter J. Burghardt, ed. *Woman: New Dimensions* (New York: Paulist Press, 1977), p. 40.
5. Faith questions even its own presuppositions and assumptions but only in order to clarify and reclaim them. The truth of faith can be maintained only through an unceasing struggle to lay hold of this truth.
6. Elizabeth Dodson Gray, *Patriarchy as a Conceptual Trap* (Wellesley, Mass.: Roundtable Press, 1982), p. 72. See Peter L. Berger, *The Sacred Canopy* (New York: Doubleday, 1967).
7. Cited in John Patrick Diggins, *The Lost Soul of American Politics* (New York: Basic Books, 1984), p. 201.

8. Irving Kristol, *Reflections of a Neoconservative* (New York: Basic Books, 1983), p. 165.

9. Max Stackhouse, *Creeds, Society and Human Rights: A Study in Three Cultures* (Grand Rapids: Eerdmans, 1984), p. 115.

10. Richard John Neuhaus, *The Naked Public Square* (Grand Rapids: Eerdmans, 1984), p. 239.

11. *Ibid.*

12. Rosemary Ruether, *Sexism and God-Talk* (Boston: Beacon Press, 1983), p. 79.

13. In an address in Ciudad Guayana, Venezuela. *Des Moines Register* (30 January, 1985), p. 6A.

14. Reinhold Niebuhr, *Christian Realism and Political Problems* (New York: Charles Scribner's Sons, 1953), p. 98.

# FIVE

# Churches under the Judgment of God

*Bruce Yocum*

IN THE PAST YEAR OR SO, the pages of the *London Times* have, occasionally, given attention to a controversy over the appointment of a bishop in the Church of England. David Jenkins, appointed in 1984 to the see of Durham, has been very forthcoming about his lack of faith in orthodox Christianity. Indeed, the basic doctrines of Christianity to which the Reverend Jenkins does not assent make quite a list. Upon his nomination, the archbishop of Canterbury declined to consecrate him, and the archbishop of York undertook the task. The consecration took place in York Catherdral on July 6, 1984. Two days after the consecration ceremony, in weather unpromising for such displays, a bolt of lightning hit York Cathedral and burned the south transept.

Because it was a topic of some considerable interest, a high-ranking churchman in the Church of England was subsequently asked, "Do you see in this the judgment of God?" The churchman said, "Well, you know that I personally disagree with the views of the bishop of Durham, but I don't believe that God intervenes in the world in that way. I don't believe that we could label any natural occurrence of that sort as a judgment of God."

It is at least a provoking sequence of events. Was the Anglican churchman right in saying that God does not intervene in this world in acts of judgment? Or, even if we stop short of pronouncing a verdict on whether this was an act of God's judgment, would we be right in finding the occurence at York Minster something to sober us and make us fear? Does God intervene in acts of judgment in this life, and does he make his judgment clear to us so that we can see it and understand it?

Christian revelation clearly teaches that God judges ultimately and that we will not escape his judgment. The conclusion of the judgment of the nations will be that the wicked "will go away into eternal punishment but the righteous into eternal life" (Mt 25:46). Paul tells us:

> For he will render to every man according to his works: to those who by patience in well-doing seek for glory and honor and immortality, he will give eternal life; but for those who are factious and do not obey the truth, but obey wickedness, there will be wrath and fury. There will be tribulation and distress for every human being who does evil, the Jew first and also the Greek, but glory and honor and peace for everyone who does good, the Jew first and also the Greek. For God shows no partiality. (Rom 2:6-11)

God intends our anticipation of his final judgment to be a powerful deterrent to wrongdoing. Jesus said, "Do not fear those who kill the body, but cannot kill the soul; rather, fear him who can destroy both soul and body in hell" (Mt 10:28). This deterrent power of fear of God can make a crucial difference in our lives. It is best to obey God out of love and conviction, but sometimes fear doesn't hurt. There are times when our love and conviction may not be sufficient, and fear prevents us from sinning. A friend of mine described to me how, through a series of circumstances, he found himself in a situation with a woman who clearly wanted to draw him into sin. He was powerfully tempted. "At the time," he said, "I didn't think much about the love of God. But I did think about God's judgment. I said to her, 'Lady, I don't know what *I* think, but I'm afraid of what *God* thinks, and I'm leaving.'"

In many churches, the judgment of God is not discussed nearly so much nowadays as in the past. I thank God that I was raised early enough in my own church to have heard a considerable amount about it when I was a child. As a consequence I can look back on my life and identify many things I am now very glad I did not do, which I did not do because of fear of God.

The reward for the righteous and the penalty for the wicked are not always experienced in this life. It would be a mistake simply to equate happiness, peace, and prosperity in this life with the blessing of God, and poverty, difficulty, and pain with the disfavor of God. Blessings come to those who follow the Lord, but we should not confuse the blessings of God with what we owe to an economic system, to a political approach, or to business practices, which may or may not be just. When we are prosperous and happy, we should ask ourselves whether we are feeling good because of the benefits of an unjust social system, or because rapacious business practices have lined our pockets abundantly, or because we are living as disciples and experiencing the blessing of God. If we are undergoing difficulty or trial or pain, is it because we have fallen out of God's favor, or is it because we have come into the tribulation that Jesus promised to those who follow Him? If we realize that God's punishment and reward are not fully handed out in this life, we can avoid the temptation to lose faith when we see the prosperity of the wicked. The psalmist said, "Behold, these are the wicked; always at ease, they increase in riches. All in vain have I kept my heart clean and washed my hands in innocence. For all the day long I have been stricken, and chastened every morning" (Ps 73:12-14). But while we may not always see God's judgment in this life, we know that he will reward the righteous and punish the wicked. If he withholds his judgment now, he is not overlooking wrongdoing. Rather, he is giving the wicked an opportunity to repent.

Nevertheless, despite these qualifications, God does intervene in this life to execute judgment.

Scripture provides us with striking examples of God's judgment. In chapter twenty-eight of the book of Jeremiah, we find Hananiah prophesying peace and prosperity, in contradiction to Jeremiah, who was prophesying woe and doom. Hananiah was much more popular than Jeremiah; a lot of people preferred his prophecies. In a sense, Jeremiah was more limited than Hananiah. All Jeremiah had to work with was the inspiration of the Holy Spirit. He could not make up clever prophecies, as Hananiah did.

Jeremiah, inspired by God, put on a wooden yoke and said, "Thus will you be enslaved in the yoke of the king of Babylon if you do not repent." Hananiah, in a seemingly brilliant stroke, stripped the yoke from Jeremiah's shoulders, broke it in pieces, and said, "Thus says the Lord, 'So will I break the yoke of the king of Babylon, and you will be saved.'" Jeremiah, astonished at this, turned to him and said, "Listen, Hananiah, the Lord has not sent you, and you have made this people believe a lie. Therefore, thus says the Lord: 'Behold, I will remove you from the face of the earth. This very year you will die. You have uttered rebellion against the Lord.'" And in that very year, in the seventh month, the prophet Hananiah died.

There are many other stories of God's judgment in the Old Testament—from the tower of Babel and Sodom and Gomorrah, through Eli and Saul and David, to the destruction of the kingdoms of Israel and Judah. The descriptions of God's judgment in this life continue in the New Testament, in dramatic incidents involving Ananias and Sapphira, Elymas the magician, Herod Antipas, and in Jesus' prediction of the destruction of Jerusalem.

God intervenes to judge individuals, nations, peoples. If we focus on God's judgment among those who are called his people, the Christian people throughout the world, we can see three reasons why he intervenes: He judges us to purify and cleanse us, removing those who stubbornly rebel against him. He judges his people to chastise and discipline us and to inspire fear of himself and of his word. And he intervenes in judgment to exercise his direct government over his people. These are not mutually exclusive purposes.

We see the first of these aspects of God's judgment in the words of the prophet Ezekiel:

> As I live, says the Lord God, surely, with a mighty hand and an outstretched arm, and with wrath poured out, I will be king over you. I will bring you out from the peoples and gather you out of the countries where you are scattered, with a mighty hand and an outstretched arm, and with wrath poured out; and I will bring you into the wilderness of the peoples, and there I will enter into judgment with you face to face. As I entered into judgment with your fathers in the wilderness of the land of Egypt, so I will enter into judgment with you, says the Lord God. I will make you pass under the rod, and I will let you go in by number. I will purge out the rebels from among you, and those who transgress against me; I will bring them out of the land where they sojourn, but they shall not enter the land of Israel. Then you will know that I am the Lord.
>
> (Ez 20:33-38)

God does not always purge out the rebels from among his people in this life; remember the parable of the tares and the wheat. There are evils that remain until the final day of judgment. But God does at times enter into judgment with his people to cure the rebellion that we are unable to cure. When he does, it is a terrible cure.

A familiar passage in Hebrews speaks of God's second purpose in judgment—intervention to instruct, chastise, and inspire fear in us. "My son, do not regard lightly the discipline of the Lord, nor lose courage when you are punished by him.

For the Lord disciplines him whom he loves and chastises every son whom he receives." First Corinthians 11:27-32 gives an instance of such judgment for discipline and chastisement. The passage shows that there is a relation between God intervening to instruct us and his creating in us a healthy fear. The relation is also illustrated in the story of Ananias and Sapphira in the fifth chapter of Acts. Ananias and Sapphira are struck down by God for their double-dealing. Not surprisingly, "great fear fell upon all those who heard of it."

God's intervention to exercise his direct government over his people can be seen in Ezekiel in God's contentions with his people, as when he says of them, "You said I want to be like the nations around us. And God says, 'As I live, you will not be.'" When God's people so turn away in their hearts that they desire to be like the surrounding nations, God says, "I am king over you. You are my people. You will not be like those nations. And if your heart is set on it, then I will have to act to bring you back."

Knowing that God does intervene in judgment of his people, we come to the question whether we can identify his judgment when it happens. Or is God's judgment in this life so difficult to discern that, for all practical purposes, our belief in it makes no difference at all?

I think that the process of discernment is reasonably accessible to us. At least to some extent, God wants us to recognize his judgment of his people. The prophets in the Old and New Testament spoke about God's judgment through revelation, through the inspiration of the Holy Spirit. God was revealing his mind to us on some important things. The Holy Spirit is with us to share the mind of Christ with us and enable us to perceive God's actions in the world. The Spirit declares to us what is Christ's so that, like Christ, we may see what the Father is doing in the world to execute judgment and bring salvation.

One of the ways we experience this operation of the Holy Spirit is by our applying what we know of God to what we know of the situations around us. God has revealed a great part of his mind to us through his word. We do not live in ignorance of the bases on which he makes his judgments. Thus we are able to form analyses of what we see that enable us to identify situations that are under God's judgment.

An example of this was a statement—an extraordinary sort of statement these days, although it should not be so extraordinary—made in *Pastoral Renewal* a few years ago. Dr. James I. Packer said, "I am forced to believe that the Church of England is under judgment these days for multiple unfaithfulness to the gospel." It may take a certain amount of courage to say it, but does it take very much discernment to believe it? The statement does not mean a rejection of God's people in the Church of England. Far from it. Perhaps if God did not love them, he would not take the time to discipline and judge and chastise them.

I was recently very encouraged by a book by Charles Habib Malik, called *A Christian Critique of the University.* Dr. Malik is a Greek Orthodox, a Lebanese, and a world-class scholar. He says in his introduction that he wanted to call the book, *What Does Jesus Christ Think of the Modern University?* He acknowledges that that method of examining the university might seem farfetched to some. But Malik replies that Jesus Christ is a real person, not just an idea, and we should want to know what he thinks of the university. What else would a Christian critique of the university mean? Malik asks. Don't we believe we can determine what Jesus Christ does think? Malik undertakes to look at the modern university from the eyes of Jesus Christ and to make judgments about it. Is that undertaking too much? Hasn't God revealed enough of his mind to us to be able to do that? If we can't do that, how could we ever propose to have a Christian university? We would not know what to make of it.

Malik carries out his project in a very convincing manner. He takes what God has revealed of his mind and applies it to what he sees, and says, "God says thus and such about these institutions." Malik helps us identify God's judgment of the modern university. I think that very often what we are lacking in discerning God's judgment in this way is not the requisite discernment or revelation or wisdom but rather conviction and courage.

I am personally convinced that God is about something in these days which is very significant, which will result in a great change in his people. He is judging his people to save many of them from destruction, both those whose teaching leads his people astray and those who follow: seducers and those seduced, deceivers and those deceived. It is obvious that there are many Christians being led into doubt or rejection of the basic teachings of the Christian faith and into unrighteous behavior by those who are in a position to teach and lead them. God wants to save those being lied to. He is acting and will act in judgment of his people to make his mind and word clear so that those who are being seduced can be saved. God also is acting and will act in judgment to save the seducers and deceivers. We can be sure that God loves them and wants to call them back.

If we look at what is happening in Western societies, it would be naive not to think that Christians may well face greater hostility, more open opposition, more serious attempts to limit our freedom to live as Christians and proclaim the gospel. I believe that God is judging his people and purifying his people to prepare us to meet these difficulties.

I also believe that God is working among his people and is ruling over them through his judgments to prepare his people for the task of global evangelism. The world is growing at such a rate that even to imagine preaching the gospel to all those on the face of the earth today is staggering. God is going to have to do something with us if we are going to be able to effectively proclaim the gospel to the nations on the earth today.

God is intervening in these ways, exercising his judgment over us, to purify us and prepare us. Insofar as any of us have any responsibility for God's people—whether it be because of a position that we have in a church or simply because of the influence that we have through the gifts that God has given us—to that degree we have a responsibility to proclaim that the judgment of God falls on those who fail to believe the gospel that he has revealed or who live in unrighteousness. It is a duty that God imposes on those to whom he gives authority and to whom he gives gifts. When we recognize situations that are under God's judgment and perceive his intervention to judge his people, we have the responsibility to proclaim his judgment. The prophets in the Old and New Testament declared God's judgment by saying, "This is what God is going to do: He will judge an institution like this if it does not change."

This is the responsibility God spoke of to Ezekiel:

> At the end of seven days, the word of the Lord came to me. 'Son of man, I have made you a watchman for the house of Israel. Whenever you hear a word from my mouth, you shall give them warning from me. If I say to the wicked, You shall surely die and you give him no warning, nor speak to warn the wicked from his wicked way, in order to save his life, he will die. But I will require his life at your hands. Again, if the righteous man turns from his righteousness and commits iniquity, and I lay a stumbling block before him, he shall die. Because you have not warned him he shall die. And I will require his life at your hands.' (Ez 3:16-20)

I believe this is one of our duties as leaders among the Christian people today. God is actively at work among the Christian people to judge us and to change us, and we who have responsibilities of leadership should help his people perceive his judgment and respond to him.

A newly appointed Catholic bishop, who must have pondered Ezekiel 3, wrote recently: "When I was given the position of authority, I started to inquire of those being trained for ministry what was being taught by their teachers of moral theology. One simple question I asked was, 'Do your teachers teach that fornication is serious sin?' In all the schools of theology the best answer I could get was from one teacher who said that it is serious sin, but that he couldn't judge. He said that if a boy and a girl have intercourse and they are in love, well, he wouldn't judge them, because our Lord said we're not supposed to judge.

"You always hear that said—'I have not come to judge.' They forget the rest, where Jesus said, 'I don't need to judge; my words will judge them.' Let's remember the words of the Lord who says in effect that if you practice fornication you will die.

"So often people take that one word, 'We shouldn't judge.' I remember one time some bishops from a European country came to me. They had written a document on abortion which began by saying that we shouldn't judge. And I said, 'You might as well turn in your resignation. One of the three duties of a bishop is to judge. He has to teach, he has to give the sacraments, and he has to judge. You have to pronounce judgment so that the people will know what is right and what is wrong. It doesn't mean we have to condemn. We leave that to God. But we do have to affirm the judgment of God.'"

Another bishop I know was just appointed to an important see. He knew that his diocese was becoming theologically confused. Early on, he sat down in a meeting where his advisors were discussing what the diocese was going to teach about sexual ethics. The gist of the conversation was, "Well, we can't really say very much. We don't know that much with certainty." He sat there feeling uncomfortable—afraid, he says candidly, to speak. He was a new bishop. He had to establish himself and win confidence.

But then he thought about God. What was God going to say to him about his diocese? So he spoke up and he said, "You know, I do think there are a few things we can say with some certainty. Adultery is wrong, for example. Practicing homosexuality is wrong. Let's just begin with those things." Well, the whole conversation changed. He discovered that most of the people on his staff believed traditional Christian teaching and were relieved that someone had had the courage to lead them in saying it.

Do these bishops' examples have something to teach us? Each of us should examine ourselves regarding whether we are proclaiming the judgments of God on wrongdoing. We should ask ourselves why so many of God's people are not afraid to sin today. Why are so many of God's people today not afraid to promote their novel opinions about Christian truth? Why is there so little fear of God? It is not hard to understand, if the judgment of God is never proclaimed.

"When thy judgments are in the earth, the inhabitants of the world learn righteousness" (Is 26:9). If favor is shown to the wicked, he will not learn to be righteous. If favor is shown to a man or a woman who teaches people to sin and not fear judgment, if favor is shown to a man or a woman who speculates freely about the Christian gospel without fear, if favor is shown to them by leaving them in positions of authority, by not speaking out against what they say—because "after all they are good people"—the wicked will not learn to be righteous.

If we believe at all in God's judgment of sin and unrighteousness, if we believe at all that God's people cannot with impunity teach something other than the gospel, then we ought to be able to proclaim that God will judge those who do such things. We do not often know when God's judgment will fall, or how it will fall, but we know that God will judge those who do such things. As the passage from Ezekiel 3 makes clear, God's judgment on those who fail to give warning when they have been given the responsibility to warn is perhaps the most severe of all. If we have positions of responsibility or influence and have not spoken out on God's behalf, fear of God ought to motivate us to some action.

But is it harsh to proclaim the judgment of God against those who do evil? Does it betray a lack of love? Is it simply prophecy of doom?

At times it is harsh because at times it is necessary to speak harshly to show people that they are dealing with something serious. But to pronounce God's judgment is much less harsh than what will happen if those who sin are not warned to turn back from their sin. Do we believe that God's judgment will fall on those who do unrighteousness? If so, why is it being harsh to say to them clearly and straightforwardly that what they are talking about is bondage and not freedom? Is it harsh—or is it only the medicine that fits the case?

To those who would speak to God's people of God intervening in judgment, I would offer three paradigms from the prophets. The first is Jeremiah. He proclaimed and proclaimed during forty long years to a people who would not listen. At the end—greatest irony of all—the people asked him for a word from the Lord concerning whether they should flee to Egypt, and he said, "No! To those few of you remaining in the land, no, don't go to Egypt"; but they went anyway and took him with them, and he died in Egypt. Jeremiah lived in anguish because of his love for God's people—not an anguish born of anger or hatred but the anguish of the bitterness that comes to a man who loves God's people and sees them stubbornly going their own way.

Isaiah is a second model. Isaiah prophesied to Hezekiah, and Hezekiah listened to him. As a result, God's people were reformed and saved. What is instructive about this model is the light it sheds on the tension between those who proclaim a message prophetically and those who are in authority. The two are not necessarily in conflict. Sometimes they have worked together, both cooperating with the Lord.

The third paradigm is the prophet Jonah. Jonah did not want to prophesy; he went to great lengths to avoid it. When he finally did prophesy, he did not put himself into it. He meandered through the city, saying verbatim the things he was given to say but not making a great attempt to win people over because he did not believe they would respond. But lo and behold, the people of Nineveh repented. The judgment of God that he so harshly proclaimed did not fall because they heeded the word of the watchman and turned back from their evil ways.

If we are faithful to God in seeking to understand his ways and proclaim them, warning people back from the judgment that rightly falls on those who teach and practice unbelief and immorality—who knows but that God in his great mercy will pour into the hearts of those who hear us a spirit of repentance, of mourning, of love for him? Then, rather than seeing judgment fall, we will see the people of God restored and strengthened and brought to life in greater ways than perhaps we are capable of imagining.

# SIX

# The Meaning of Salvation: Contemporary Distortions

*Harold O.J. Brown*

I WOULD LIKE TO SPEAK TO YOU about distortions of salvation. Let me begin with an illustration from Mark's Gospel, or rather with something that seems to be missing from that Gospel, as many scholars read it. As most Bible students know, the final twelve verses of chapter sixteen are considered by many not to belong to Mark's original. There are various reasons for this view. However, it hardly seems likely that the original ended with the last verse that many scholars consider to be authentic, verse 8 of chapter 16: "And they went out quickly, and fled from the sepulchre; for they trembled and were amazed: neither said they anything to any man; for they were afraid." End of quote, end of Gospel. I don't think that this is a very good ending, nor that it is a likely one. The most frequently repeated command in the Bible is "Fear not," or "Don't be afraid." Wouldn't it be remarkable for Mark's Gospel, which many suppose to be our oldest Gospel, to conclude with the words, "For they were afraid"? Most New Testament scholars think that the present longer ending was added later. Presumably, if the familiar, traditional ending is a later addition, there was once more to chapter sixteen, now lost, so that the Gospel would not end on a note of fear.

The traditional "received text," which we have in the Authorized (King James) Version as well as in the older translations and some of the newer ones, contains one form of the Great Commission. The Great Commission, of course, we know better from Matthew 28:18-20, but Mark's form is interesting for us here. "Go ye into all the world, and preach the gospel to every creature" (Mk 16:15), or better, "to all creation." What is meant by the words "to all creation"? I submit that the words "to all creation" reflect the absolute claims of the gospel, of Jesus Christ and his message. The message is not merely good news for a limited circle: it has universal significance. Christ and the gospel are not relative to time and location. Similarly, in Matthew's Gospel, we are told to "go into all the world" and to make disciples "of every nation." It may be that Mark's expression "to all creation" means no more than "to everyone," but even this limited interpretation would reflect the fact that the gospel is not something for a select group of initiates but for all of mankind. Even if Mark did not specifically mean "all creation," we can say that if the message of the Bible is true, if the incarnation, the crucifixion, the resurrection and all the rest are indeed objective truth and not merely religious poetry, then the gospel message necessarily has a cosmic dimension and possesses implications for all of reality, that is, for all creation. The gospel is the story of the eternal Word of God, the divine Logos, "without whom nothing was made that was made" (Jn 1:3).

Consequently, there is a sense in which the gospel is not "good news" merely for humans who believe it but also for the whole of creation, for the entire cosmos, as Paul says in Romans 8:20-22. There we learn that the entire creation is groaning with longing for liberation, a longing to be set free, to enjoy "glorious liberty." Liberty in Paul's sense is indeed glorious, provided that one sees this important qualification: it is "the glorious liberty of the children of God."

Salvation is far too precious for us to misunderstand or to define in such a way that its true meaning is obscured. There are several ways that this can happen. Most of them involve, in one way or another, forgetting the words, "of God." Salvation can be distorted by failing to qualify it as "of God," or by qualifying it too much, by limiting it to one of its aspects and forgetting others. One such limitation occurs when salvation is reduced to the dimension of liberation without being specific about what one is to be liberated from, nor who is to accomplish the liberation. Salvation is freedom that comes from God. To omit the "from God" and merely to say "freedom" has given rise to a swarm of distortions. "Freedom" is right, but to say "freedom" only, out of its full biblical context, is inaccurate.

We began with a reference to the gospel "to all creation." The Bible does speak of freedom and thus of liberation, but this cannot be seen as its central content unless we make freedom a synonym for salvation. Do we bring salvation, a religious concept, closer to people when we describe it in terms of freedom, something that everyone thinks he understands? Are the two ideas interchangeable? May we identify freedom or liberation with salvation, or is there a fundamental distinction between them? Freedom is a wonderful concept, but its usual English meaning must be amplified by adding the dimension of healing or wholeness in order for the words "freedom" and "liberation" to begin to give an adequate description of what Jesus Christ has done.

Freedom, being set free, liberation is certainly an aspect of the work of Christ. But is it the whole? A number of the miracles of Jesus illustrate the fact that he brings more than mere liberating, unless we understand "liberty" in the fullest possible sense, in other words, unless we define it as including health in the full biblical sense of the word. There is a relationship between the concepts of freedom on the one hand

and health or wholeness on the other, a relationship that can clearly be seen when we ask ourselves what their opposites are. The opposite of health is death. The opposite of freedom is bondage, but from a biblical perspective it is useful to speak of freedom from that which causes bondage, namely, sin. Sometimes the biblical expressions "salvation" and "redemption" refer to one, sometimes to the other, sometimes to both. For a moment we should pause and note the relationship between the concepts of health and wholeness, both linguistically and biblically, in the languages that most of us use. English is a Germanic language, and in Germanic the word for salvation, *das Heil,* is clearly the cognate of our English word "health." *Heilen* means "to heal," and thus a physician *heilt*—he heals. The adjective *heil* means the same as the English "whole" or "safe." And we immediately note that the English adjective "safe" and the verb "to save," which come from the Latin rather than from German roots, represent essentially the same idea as healthy, whole, heal. Health, wholeness, and salvation are related concepts.

There is, however, a very important distinction between freedom or liberty on the one hand, and health or wholeness on the other. Freedom is defined in terms of a negative, of an evil; health in terms of something that is positive and good. Freedom is essentially a negative concept, defined in terms of those things that limit it. We always have to specify: "freedom from what?" or "for what?" Health and wholeness are positive concepts, defined not in terms of the absence of an evil but of conformity to a good. A mummy is free from disease, but it isn't healthy. The biblical concept of freedom, the greatest freedom, is defined in terms of the greatest enemies of freedom, which are sin and death. Only that which can liberate us from sin and death can truly make us free in the sense of John 8:36: "If the Son shall therefore make you free, ye shall be free indeed." It is important to note this distinction between the concepts of freedom as *freedom from,* and health or wholeness as *harmony with* (or *conformity to*), even as we emphasize the fact that Christ came to bring us *both*. Otherwise, we are likely to abstract salvation from its model, from remaking fallen man in the image of God, restored in Christ, and produce an empty concept of freedom, into which nonbiblical contents can be poured.

Perhaps the most dramatic example of misuse of the word "freedom" is in the expression "freedom of choice" as used in the abortion controversy. "Do you believe in freedom? If so, you must be in favor of freedom of choice." All Americans believe in freedom, or at least we are supposed to do so, and so we are all drawn to this slogan. But of course the important questions to ask are "Freedom *from* what?" and "Freedom *for* what?" Abortion means freedom *from* the restraints on killing, freedom *to* be able to kill, and this then is not such a positive concept.

Many quests for freedom limit themselves to the negative view. This may help to explain the fact that many if not all liberation theologies work to overthrow what they consider an oppressive system in total disregard for the fact that the system which in all human probability will replace it will be the even worse tyranny of totalitarianism.

But now we should turn from these general considerations based on language to some specific examples from Scripture. Consider the case of the woman afflicted for twelve years with hemorrhaging (Mk 5:25-34). Jesus tells her, "Daughter, thy faith hath made thee whole." This expression from the Authorized (King James) Version, "made thee whole," may properly be translated "has saved you" as well as "has healed you." What did Jesus mean to tell the woman? Did Jesus mean to tell her that eternal salvation, which she could not see, would be hers as well as the physical healing that she could both see and feel? Or was he merely promising a cure for her hemorrhage?

In Mark 5:34, Jesus speaks to the woman of her "faith." "Thy faith hath healed thee." Presumably at this point in his ministry, Jesus' followers did not have a highly developed faith. Peter's confession that Jesus is the promised Messiah, which is the first really explicit confession of Christian faith, will be made later, in chapter eight. If not even Peter had come to a full recognition of who Christ is, we can hardly suppose that the woman who followed him in the crowd had done so. In this case, what was her "faith"? Was it what we call "saving faith"? Probably not in the sense of trusting in the work of Christ—after all, he still had not performed its essential parts. At the very least, it involved the recognition that she would be helped by laying hold of Christ. She *did* lay hold of him, quite literally, at least of his clothes, and in fact, she *was* helped, at least for the time being. Did he mean, thy faith hath "given thee temporary relief"? He clearly did mean at least that. But what else did he mean? Or was that enough?

Let us consider another New Testament example. In the case of the paralyzed man in Mark 2, the first thing that Jesus said to him was "Your sins are forgiven"—good news, but probably not what he was hoping for. He had come for the sake of his physical health, or rather because of his lack of it. His paralysis, which is impotence, lack of potency, of power, ability to act and do, is the basic condition of fallen man. Is an allegorical answer enough for a man who is lying paralyzed on a pallet? Is mere forgiveness of sins, the wiping away of moral guilt, the cure for his paralysis? Did it restore his power? Forgiveness, like freedom, only wipes the slate clean. What are we going to write on it? To know what to write, we need a positive model. If Jesus had said only, "Your sins are forgiven," we might understand him to be saying: "I have no cure for you here, but you can have hope in the hereafter." It is important to note that Jesus did *not* limit his remarks to that, although that would have been of tremendous value, but he added: "Rise, pick up your bed, and walk!" We should note that this way of dealing with the paralyzed man has an evangelistic purpose, directed not only towards the paralytic himself but towards the hearers: "That ye may know that the Son of Man hath power on earth to forgive sins" (Mk 2:10). The paralyzed man, restored to physical health, must subsequently have died from some other cause. Liberation from this-worldly evils is temporary, and we must put it in the context of an ultimate liberation from sin and death. Nevertheless, in the New Testament this does not destroy the significance of this-worldly healing. The healing and wholeness that Jesus brings does have a this-worldly, practical, physical dimension. To fail to see this is to reduce his promise of salvation. We might call this reduction of biblical salvation that of Christian Science—a bit anachronistic, of course, but perhaps it will make the point. The gospel is not "all in the mind," and the consequences of faith are not merely mental, or in the weak sense of the word, spiritual.

On the other hand, to see only the cure for paralysis is to see far too little. Jesus said and did nothing about the man's paralysis *until* he had spoken of forgiveness of sins—and until at least the scribes and the Pharisees had gotten the message and had asked their rhetorical question: "Who can forgive sins but God alone?"

This pharisaical question is the clue to the second distortion of salvation: If the first distortion is to suggest that salvation has no physical dimension, the second is to suggest that salvation has no prolongation into eternity. The Pharisees, in effect, are saying to Jesus: "You have no right to speak of the forgiveness of sin, with its *eternal* consequences, unless you can speak for the Eternal One, the Ancient of Days, for God himself." They saw this clearly, and they were absolutely right in seeing it. They might well have accepted a mere physical healing without objection. After all, there were plenty of wonder-workers of various kinds in Palestine in those days. But a healing in the context of a claim to messianic authority, indeed, to deity, they could not and would not accept. Thus the second great distortion of salvation is that of the Pharisees. (We must overlook the quarrel between the Pharisees and the Sadducees in this context.)

And here we come to an interesting paradox. Those who believed or at least hoped that Jesus could cure them supposed that the power to cure resided in him. And they drew the logical conclusion: they went to him—were carried, in the case of the paralyzed man; actually took hold of his clothes, in the case of the hemorrhaging woman. It did not occur to them to think that simply because Jesus had the power to heal, they would be healed. They did not even think that because the man with the power to heal, the Healer, was present, not merely in the world but actually in Roman Palestine, that that was enough to insure that everyone would be healed. They went to him, spoke to him, they even grabbed him.

Surely all of us would admit relief from disease, which must be temporary in effect as long as man is mortal, is not as important as eternal salvation. And if no one seriously supposed that the presence of Jesus in Palestine with the power to heal meant ultimate physical healing and perfect health for all residents and tourists, how can we be so gullible as to suppose that the presence in the world of Jesus with the power to save, as the Savior, means ultimate salvation for all those who happen to reside here on earth? How can we suppose that his saving power, which we confess, means universal salvation, any more than his healing power meant universal healing, without respect to whether or not those who wanted to be healed sought him out and went to him?

There are quite a few distortions of salvation, although I think that the various fanciful varieties can be classified in four categories. Perhaps it will be helpful to place them in the ancient Greek categories of physics: "All is earth, air, fire and water." Perhaps this old slogan will help us to remember what I take to be the four major contemporary errors.

"All is earth": "Salvation is here and now *only*."

"All is air": "Salvation is totally spiritual (perhaps even *imaginary*, in another world, hanging in the air)."

"All is fire": "Everything that now exists will ultimately be consumed. There *is no salvation*, properly speaking." This is not really salvation at all.

"All is water": "Everything comes out in the wash. Everyone will be saved!"

Let us consider these four distortions in alphabetical order: air, earth, fire and water. "All is air," we can call the distortion of Gnosticism. Gnosticism is out of date, so we can call it the distortion of Christian Science. But Christian Science comes from Boston and may seem a little esoteric to us here in the Middle West. So I shall take a risk and say that it is sometimes the distortion of pietistic evangelicalism. "All is earth" salvation is here and now, which is all that counts. We may call this the theology of Pharisaism, or, to be more contemporary, of liberation theology. "All is fire," we can call materialism—the prevailing view of tough-minded modern man. "All is water" we shall call universalism, the concept that all will be saved. Even tough-minded people often become sentimental when faced with the death of someone they love, or with their own death.

1. *All is air:* Salvation lies entirely in the realm of the spirit. This is the theology of the saving of souls. For the saving of souls, there is ample New Testament authority—in the King James version: "For what is a man profited, if he shall gain the whole world, and lose his own soul?" (Mt 16:26). However, if we look more closely, we see that what the King James translators render as "soul" really means "life." It is not a question of mere "spiritual" or soul survival but of saving the human being. The concept of "lostness" includes the whole man, as King James's men make plain in Matthew 10:28: "Fear not them which kill the body, but are not able to kill the soul: but rather fear him which is able to destroy both body and soul in hell." Damnation involves the destruction of both body and soul; it is more reasonable to hold that salvation involves the restruction—or, more biblically, the resurrection—of the body as well as the survival of the soul. My great Orthodox teacher Georges Flovosky was fond of saying: "One can be a

Christian and not believe in the immortality of the soul, but one cannot be a Christian and not believe in the resurrection of the body." (Of course, he had in mind the Platonic, philosophical idea that the soul is an incorruptible entity, one which naturally must continue to live after death.) The Christian's hope of eternal life is sound and solid, but it does not depend on the spiritual quality of the soul. It depends on the creating and redeeming activity of the living God. This is a very important distinction.

"All is air" we may call the theology of the beautiful island of somewhere. Whatever happens to this mortal body, the soul is indestructible. This is not biblical. It is not Christian. It is pre-Christian, Platonic, and post-Christian, neo-Platonic, Gnostic, the rational "necessary postulate" of practical reason, according to Immanuel Kant, the idealism of Fichte, the Christian Science of Mary Baker Eddy. The idea that the soul is independent of the body and has a destiny unrelated to that of the body lends itself to the doctrine of reincarnation, which has always been a temptation, even for Christians, who ought to know better. It arises thus: The soul is indestructible. However, human beings have to have bodies to be real. So we are tempted to suppose that when one body wears out and is cast aside, the indestructible soul must take upon itself another body. I see this idea of the reincarnation of an immortal soul as one of the great religious temptations to modern men and women in North America and Europe.

2. *All is earth:* According to this opposite doctrine, what is important is what happens here and now, or what is going to happen in the foreseeable future, right here on earth. To this concept, we would oppose the words of Paul. "If in this life only we have hope in Christ, we are of all men most miserable" (1 Cor 15:19). I am sure that Paul, often derided as a patriarchal male chauvinist, would include women in this warning about misery. This heresy, "all is earth," we may call that of liberation theology, or more facetiously, that of

"immanentizing the eschaton." It actually involves two errors, a major one and a minor one. The major heresy is Marxism, which denies the reality of the spiritual, the ideal, the intellectual: "The brain secretes thought as the liver secretes bile." The only reality, the only thing that is important to us, is here-and-now material reality, and the only thing that the gospel can mean when it talks about salvation is a transformation in social and economic structure. There are two problems with this view: the first, that it is theologically wrong, and the second, that it doesn't work.

It is a curious fact that so many of those who are enthusiastic for liberation theology ignore what ought to be an evident fact, one underlined by the late President Charles de Gaulle of France, who called for "a way to alleviate the evils of consumer society that does not fasten on us the most odious tyrannies ever known to man." Unfortunately, most people do not heed his warning but are perfectly willing to destroy an existing, faulty social order even though it means supplanting it with an odious Marxist tyranny.

The minor heresy of this type I call "late great planetary theology," namely, the idea that the full realization of God's purposes here on earth must be predictable within a definite time frame. By the early 1980s, *The Late, Great Planet Earth* had already sold seventeen million copies. It has had an amazing appeal. To be able to state definitely when prophecies will be fulfilled, when we can expect complete liberation (in the New Testament, not the Marxist sense) seems wonderful. If one points out that Jesus told his disciples, "It is not for you to know the times and the seasons," we may note that the book's author, Hal Lindsay, was not one of them, so perhaps it *is* for him to know. The point that we should make here is one that was emphasized by John Theodore Mueller, the late Missouri Synod Lutheran theologian, who attributes much of the eagerness to know the precise details about the return of Christ to an unwillingness to accept the humble state of the church here and now.

The major heresy, Marxism, takes the future totally out of God's hands; the minor one sees it as under God's control but makes far too much of knowing the exact timetable, of being able to foresee when and how God's purposes will be worked out, here, for us. While this does not bring it under our control, in a sense we can say that it brings it under our "supervision."

**3. *All is fire:*** If "all is earth" is a materialistic creed of salvation, "all is fire" is a materialist creed of no salvation. The *Bhagavad-Gita* of this materialism is Carl Sagan's book, *Cosmos*, which begins with the sentence, "All that is, all that ever was, and all that ever will be, is the cosmos." The cosmos is much bigger and grander than the earth, but like the earth, it is all created— it does not exist itself but through the will of the Creator. To Sagan's concept we oppose again the words of Paul, "If in this life only we have hope in Christ, we are of all men most miserable." The materialist doctrine is an incredible reductionism, one in which many people take confidence because they fear the consequences of their sinful lives. "It is appointed unto men once to die" is as far as they want to read in Hebrews 9:27; the words that follow are uncomfortable: "but after this the judgment." Convinced that there is no such thing as a soul distinct from the body, they refuse to conceive that the death of the body is anything but final.

To this doctrine, "all is fire," I would oppose two caveats: one speculative but provocative of thought, the other biblical and provocative of fear. As R.L. Bruckberger writes, "Les plus misérables d'entre nous sont ceux qui n'attendent rien et le proclament bien haut avec une sorte de satisfaction hautaine, comme un eunuque serait fier d'être chatré" ("The most miserable among us are those who do not expect anything and who loudly proclaim it with a sort of supercilious smugness, like a eunuch proud of being castrated." [R.L. Bruckberger, *La révélation de Jésus Christ* (Paris: Grasset, 1983), p. 182.])What Bruckberger has in mind is what many of us sense when we deal with people who deny all awareness that there is anything beyond this mortal life. We have the feeling that we are confronting a kind of spiritual mutilation. Bruckberger's analogy is not bad.

Do we really expect nothing? This is the situation with much of the modern church—Catholic, Protestant, not to mention Jews—which expects God to do nothing at all, or, if possible, even less. If this world is all that there is, then we should agree with Paul that we are "most miserable."

There is a second caveat to the "all is fire": "It is appointed unto men once to die, but after this the judgment" (Heb 9:27). There is an important once-for-all event, death, and a terribly important once-for-all event that follows it— judgment, not reincarnation. The Negro spiritual says, "You've got to stand your test in the Judgment, you've got to stand it all alone." That isn't quite true: You have to stand it on your own, but not all alone because if you stand it with Christ, then you will pass it: "There is therefore now no condemnation to them which are in Christ Jesus" (Rom 8:1). We cannot count on the fire to consume us, at least not before the judgment. The "all is fire" concept cannot furnish a psychological escape clause, as it seems to many to do: "It doesn't matter what we do, because in the last analysis, we will no longer exist."

**4. *All is water:*** We have already discussed this final view of salvation. There was a picture on the cover of a recent German illustrated magazine of a group of naked people on a beach, with the caption: "Das Meer wascht alles Uebel ab," the sea washes all evil away. I did not read the article, and so I do not know how this idea was developed, but I think that you can see that this is a sort of popular manifestation of the theological illusion that is widespread—especially in German-speaking Switzerland, where I work—"Everything will turn out all right, God is a loving God, all will be saved." Universalism or universal salvation, the doctrine that all will ultimately be saved, is a kind of excuse for ineffectiveness or inactivity in evangelism. We often speak of two kinds of universal salvation, "unitarian" and "universalist." The unitarian view is: God is so good that he would not damn anyone; the universalist: We are so good that God would not dare damn us. We can call this a kind of "theology of the Red Queen." In *Alice in Wonderland*, the Red Queen supervised a highly disorganized kind of race, which ended in total confusion. Asked, "Who won?" she replied, "All have won, and all must receive prizes!" I think that universalism, the last of our errors, is a theology of despair, that is, of non-hope. We do not really expect or hope we can win the world, or even a substantial number of the people in it, for Christ, and so we say, "It really doesn't matter. Everyone will be saved anyhow. All is water."

In conclusion, the distortions of salvation are sometimes totalizing, sometimes reductionist, sometimes both at the same time. Salvation is reduced to one of its aspects: air (spiritual survival), earth (politico-economic liberation), fire (nothing at all will be saved), or water (everything will be saved). Each of these errors is based on human reason. Each of them has a measure of plausibility, but not even the best of them is adequate. The great temptation of the church at the end of the twentieth century is not to deny salvation but to falsify it and to do so in a way that is consistent with the appeal of human reason.

I began with the idea, "All is earth, air, fire and water," drawn from Greek philosophy. The philosophical, economic, and psychological reductions of salvation are inadequate. When we rely too much on human reason, we come out with folly. "The foolishness of God is wiser than men" (1 Cor 1:25). It is true that we can seek to analyze salvation, to break it up into some of its component parts, to see what it means for various aspects of reality, but it is much more important to see the whole of what God graciously offers us: He offers us freedom, including perhaps temporary freedom from oppression in this world, but most certainly freedom from the greatest of all evils, sin and death and their ultimate consequence, damnation. He offers healing, eternal good health, if we may put it thus, not merely physical health in the here-and-now but resurrection life: "We shall be like him; for we shall see him as he is" (1 Jn 3:2). The whole creation is waiting for liberty, but for liberty of a very special kind: the glorious liberty of the children of God. "To all who received him, who believed in his name, he gave power to become children of God" (Jn 1:12; RSV).

# SEVEN

# The Lures and Limits of Political Power

*Charles W. Colson*

T HE PLACE OF RELIGION IN AMERICAN LIFE, particularly political life, emerged as one of the hottest issues of the 1984
presidential campaign. The topic was not only a major item in
the statements and speeches of the candidates but also received
more attention per square inch in the editorial pages than at
any other time in recent history.

Consider the following:

President Reagan announced to 17,000 cheering conven-
tion delegates in Dallas that "without God, democracy will not
and cannot long endure." Only days earlier Ms. Ferraro had
questioned God's place in the President's agenda: "The
President walks around calling himself a good Christian, but I
don't believe it for one minute, because [his] policies are so
terribly unfair."

The Catholic Archbishop of New York followed up by
suggesting what he took to be the duty of a "good Christian"
in the political sphere—"I don't see how a Catholic in good
conscience can vote for a candidate who explicitly supports
abortion"—and thereby, implicitly at least, questioned the
Christian conscience of two prominent prochoice Catholic

officeholders—Ferraro and Governor Cuomo of New York.

Then Mondale vigorously attacked the President's public statements, arguing that "in America, our faith has always been intensely personal." Thus, saith he, according to our founding fathers, "religion [in the United States] would be *here* . . . and the politicians would be over *there*—and we'd never get the two mixed up."

Throughout the campaign, fundamentalist ministers, partially at the instigation of Sen. Paul Laxalt's "Dear Christian Leader" letter, were energetically organizing massive voter registration campaigns in conservative churches and offering guidance through "Presidential Biblical Scorecards."

As these illustrations suggest, the 1984 electoral struggle began to sound more like a holy crusade than a political campaign.

Many Americans were uncomfortable with this, questioning whether it is proper to involve the Almighty in the election. Others were understandably confused by God's purported spokesmen advocating so many conflicting paths to political heaven; can it be that God speaks with a forked tongue?

Compounding the problem was the fact that this issue, having been neglected for so long by the purveyors of public discourse, suffered greatly from a lack of understanding or consensus with regard to the meaning of the terms employed in the discussion and a lack of a general apprehension of appropriate rules for debate.

Richard John Neuhaus pointed out that particularly with the return of evangelicals from the "wilderness to which they had been consigned by the educational, media, and mainline religious leadership," religiously grounded values were reintroduced in a manner quite disconcerting to those who had gloried in the secularization of American public life. The crisis, Neuhaus argued, was that "we do not have the vocabulary to debate moral issues in the public square." And this, Neuhaus warned, "could be severely damaging, if not fatal, to the American democratic experiment."

I agree. And so, for my part, I would like to offer some small contribution toward exposing a few of the red herrings which many drag across the path of discourse, distorting what little vocabulary we do have. Then I will attempt to deal with an even greater concern: that the confusion of the day has led otherwise perceptive persons to miss the central danger arising from the present revival of religion in political life, the danger that by adopting one or another of the politicized options in the contemporary discussion, the cutting edge of historic Christian witness to Jesus Christ will be absorbed by the secular culture.

The first "herring," a fish quite potent for putting one off the scent, is the cry heard in all parts of the land that we stand in serious danger of a "religious establishment" through the newly awakened political efforts of the religious. Thus, some, having long ago consigned religion to our unenlightened and bigoted past, see in the discussion an ominous return to the mythologies that fueled the fires of the stake for individuals and religious wars among nations.

Hand-wringing commentators solemnly warn us that the growing religious influence in politics endangers political freedom and religious pluralism. Beware of the tyranny of religion, they cry; our very structures are threatened by evangelizing presidents and right-wing power blocs. Some have been moved to hysterical comparisons, as was a *Washington Post* columnist who trembled, "I would rather take my chances with your average atheist than, say, the Reverend Jerry Falwell. I grant you, he is religious. But so, too, is the Ayatollah."

Such editorializing notwithstanding, can anyone seriously suppose that a government-imposed religious establishment will arise, phoenix-like, from the fractured and chaotic manifestation of Christianity in the United States? Is there a danger of the "Christianizing" of America? Consider: within Protestantism, denominationalism has run amuck, with new groupings appearing and disappearing almost as quickly as pop stars and space movies. The Roman Catholic church, once a well-ordered and stately ship, has been tossed since Vatican II on the turbulent seas of division and dissent that formerly were the characteristic mark of its Protestant offspring.

Evangelicalism, always a frail coalition of mixed doctrinal parentage, is now racked by a hot debate concerning one of its few cardinal doctrines: the inerrancy of Scripture. And the fundamentalists, for all their supposed political punch, are fiercely independent when it comes to doctrinal matters, unable and, in principle, unwilling to be bound and united by a common creed.

Add to this mix the majority in our culture who are bored by, and indifferent to, religion, and a minority who are passionately and bitterly opposed to it. Overall consider the individualistic bent that seems to be genetically fixed as a part of our national character, and one is hard pressed to understand, let alone be moved by, the near hysterical concern that the current prominence of religion in national politics forbodes government establishment of religion and the loss of our civil liberties. Such a thought is literally incredible.

The second "herring" is not so much a false scent as it is an attempt to cut off the nose altogether. Never have so many labored over the so-called "wall of separation" between church and state in order to rebuke the political preachers. What nonsense. To suggest that the "wall of separation," if there be such a wall, was erected to keep religion out of politics is to utterly misunderstand the dynamic forces at work in the founding of the republic.

Let me explain. Though the early Christians had little opportunity to face the issue of church and state, with the conversion of Constantine the terms of the debate radically changed. In turning himself and the Roman empire to Christianity at the beginning of the fourth century, Constantine brought into sharp focus the question of the relation between the church (the Christian church) and the state (the

"Christian" state). In many ways the history of Western social and political thought is defined by the outworking of one or the other of two powerful ideas: the church ascendent over the state, or, the state ascendent over the church.

With the founding of the American republic, however, an entirely new position was forged. As in so many other ways, the new American experience led to a unique American experiment: the separation of church and state. Since the time of Constantine, in no part of Christendom, and by no branch of the Christian church, had it been agreed that the state and the church should be separate and independent bodies.

The basis of this radical idea was found in the convergence of at least two, frequently conflicting, sources. First, some of the founders were clearly gripped by the Enlightenment confidence that public virtue was possible without religion as its foundation. The God hypothesis was no longer necessary in the moral sphere any more than it was in the natural sphere.

Second, and more significant for our purposes, was the growing conviction on the part of Christians that in biblical teaching the church had been given by Christ its own structure, officers, terms of admission, and so on, for the promotion and extension of true religion through the preaching of the gospel. Conversely, the Scriptures were thought to teach that the state was ordained in God's providence with its own structures, officers, and terms of admission for a quiet and peaceable public order, through pains and penalties threatened and imposed on those who disrupt that order.

The conclusion was manifest. Church and state, having differing ends, and differing means suited to those ends, ought not be confounded or confused. In its full flower the notion of separation of church and state grew out of Christian conviction that the church was built only by the conversion of men and women—conversion grounded in individual conscience, wrought by a sovereign and supernatural work of God upon the soul. Thus the state could, in principle, neither successfully establish nor destroy the church, since the state could not rule the conscience and could not transform the souls of men and women. The statement of Baptist minister Isaac Backus (1724-1806) is representative: "Religion is a concern between God and the soul with which no human authority can intermeddle."

Thus, at the founding of the republic, two naturally mortal enemies, the Enlightenment and the Christian faith, found some common ground on American soil. Both agreed that the new government should neither establish nor interfere with the church. The clause on religious liberty in the Virginia Declaration of Rights (1776) sums up the thinking of our Founding Fathers succinctly:

> That religion, or the duty we owe to our Creator, and the manner of discharging it, can be directed only by reason and conviction, not by force or violence, and therefore all men are equally entitled to the free exercise of religion, according to the dictates of conscience; and that it is the mutual duty of all to practice Christian forbearance, love, and charity toward each other.

Yet so far from there being a wall of separation between *religion* and the state, by this separation of *church* and state, the Founding Fathers recognized that, given the nature of the Christian religion, the values of a professedly Christian people would play an intimate and vital role in the formulation of public policy.

John Adams acknowledged this truth when he argued, in 1798, that:

> We have no government armed in power capable of contending in human passions unbridled by morality and religion. Our Constitution was made only for a moral and religious people. It is wholly inadequate for the government of any other.

Our Christian forefathers did not capitulate to the Enlightenment dream of reason alone as the basis for public virtue. And they witnessed the wisdom of their stand when in the French Revolution the opposing principles were played out on the stage of human history. There, as liberty was achieved by "the last prince strangled with the guts of the last priest," it was demonstrated that the "dreams of reason produce monsters."

On the contrary, our fathers, for the most part, believed that if God was gracious and the church faithful to its calling, the moral foundation of the republic would be secure without a government-established church. Christians, they expected, as citizens of the republic, would actively bring their religious values to the public forum. So, George Washington could argue that:

> Of all the dispositions and habits which lead to a political prosperity, religion and morality are indispensable supports. In vain would that man claim the tribute of Patriotism, who should labor to subvert these great pillars of human happiness.

Thus, no one supposed that when laws were passed reflecting the consensus of Christian values in the land, that thereby the Christian religion was being "established," or that morality was being "imposed" on an unwilling people. From the beginning we were committed to the notion that public policy would grow out of moral consensus, regardless of whether the source of that morality was identifiably religious or not. But it is sheer nonsense to suggest that our Founding Fathers could have even conceived of the notion that all religiously grounded moral positions should be ruled out of the public sphere. The point was that such convictions could only become the law of the land if you could persuade a majority, whether they shared the religious foundation or not, that the course proposed was in fact the best course to pursue.

Our modern privatization of religion, the conception of religion as that which people do in the privacy of their own homes or churches, would have been unintelligible to the founders of the republic, even those who repudiated the Christian faith.

Our history is filled with examples of how this has worked out in practice. From the very beginning the American Revolution itself was seen by many as a rebellion fueled by the concerns of Christian obedience. Man is a creature of God before he is a creature of the state, and his political life must be conditioned by that truth. As James Madison argued in 1785:

> It is the duty of every man to render to the Creator such homage and such only as he believes to be acceptable to Him. This duty is precedent, both in order of time and degree of obligation, to the claims of Civil Society. Before any man can be considered as a member of Civil Society, he must be considered as a subject of the Governor of the Universe.

And so it has been; from the abolitionist movement of the 1860s to the civil rights movement of the 1960s, from Prohibition to public prayer, never has there been a time in the life of our nation when religiously founded values did not play an important, if not leading, role in the character of American political life.

The debate over religion and politics during the 1984 presidential campaign and since has so far failed to clarify one very important issue for Christians. The debate has seemed to pose two choices: one side arguing that faith in God and country are inseparable, a position known historically as civil religion; the other side asserting that one's religion is entirely a private matter. The public, including many Christians, have been left believing that religion's proper role in American life has to fall into one of these two politically defined alternatives. But neither of these options has anything to do with historic

Christianity—and there is the danger. Let me explain. First, let us look at the generic civil religion advocated by one camp. "Religion plays a critical role in the political life of our nation," said one candidate. What kind of religion? "If you practice a religion, whether you are Catholic, Protestant, Jewish, or guided by some other faith, then your private life will be influenced by a sense of obligation and so, too, your public life."

Thus, in the civil religionists' view, we are a "tolerant" society, "open to and encouraging of all religions." We do this because religion is the great prop of the duties of citizens. This prop is necessary because we can see that whenever a great civilization has fallen, one of the significant forerunners of the fall was its turning away from God or its gods. As a former president once argued, the American government makes no sense "unless it is founded in a deeply felt religious faith—and I don't care what it is."

Countering this view was the opposition's notion that "faith [is] intensely personal." There are many "faiths," all of which are "true" for those who hold them. To have religion enter political debates might require that a person defend his religious beliefs! What could be more uncivil?

Perhaps the best example of this kind of religion was found in New York Governor Mario Cuomo's much publicized speech at Notre Dame. There, with eloquence and sophistication, he argued that an officeholder who professes to be a sincere Christian can advocate positions clearly contrary to his church's teaching.

Thus, for example, his stated view is that as a practicing Catholic he subscribes to his church's teachings on the question of abortion. But, he argued, as an officeholder in a secular society, he could not impose his views on anyone else. So far, so good.

But Governor Cuomo did not stop there. He went on to say that he is under no obligation to advocate the views of his church or to work to seek a public consensus based on those views (which views he confesses to be the truth of God) until there is what he calls a "prudential judgment" which could justify such a course. Another way of saying this is that you do not act on a sticky question until the majority of voters agree with you. That, of course, is how you get elected and stay in office. The judgment of prudence appears to be pretty good politics.

Yet, this kind of logic, however effective as a political ploy, in my view, gives sophistry a bad name. No more do we have the claim of the Christian religion that it declares the truth of God, which alone is able to make men and women "wise unto salvation." Rather, we have a religion that is a matter of personal taste. The ancients had counsel for us in this regard: *de gustibus non est disputandum*. "There is no disputing about tastes." Thus we dare not bring faith into politics; such a course would reduce political debate to futility. How can one argue with the flavor of religion that I happen to favor?

Here generic faith is protected from public scrutiny; whatever concerns may grow out of such faith are not to be brought to the hard decisions of the political sphere. No one should attempt to transform policy debates into theological disputes. Held consistently, this view leads to the notion that it is morally possible to believe with your church that abortion is murder while supporting the practice with your vote.

In plain terms what we have today is a debate between those who believe that generic religion is a crucial prop to public morality and civic duty, and is thus to be publicly encouraged and endorsed, and those who believe that generic faith is to be privately engaging, but publicly irrelevant.

Any who fear the specter of theocracy in response to this debate wildly overrate the power of such insipid religion. Neither civil religion nor privatized religion is very likely to impose a long-lasting impact on our governmental institutions, for in both cases there is virtually nothing to impose.

One commentator seemed to get this point. She wrote longingly of ancient Rome as a model of the place that generic religion might have in a "tolerant" society: "The people regarded all the modes of worship as equally true, the intellectuals regarded them as equally false, and the politicians regarded them as equally useful. What a well-blessed time."

Of course, we Christians should know that such emptiness and cynicism has nothing to do with blessing. Yet in the heat of the presidential campaign there was a great temptation to quietly opt for one of these false paths as a way to express biblical faith.

For example, ought a candidate to have received a Christian's enthusiastic support because he supports certain religious values? What about prayer in public schools? Prayer is surely a religious act, and religion is surely advanced by such acts.

But is this Christian? The Bible teaches that the only persons who may call God Father are those *adopted* into his family through Jesus Christ; only those who are praying in the name of Christ have a right to pray to God as *Father*.

How then can a Christian be thrilled by an endorsement of general religiosity when that amounts to a denial of one of the choice benefits given only to those who are in Christ? How can we encourage a practice which leads people to believe that they may have access to the throne of God apart from Christ? Yet this appears to be exactly what we are doing in our political support for generic religion. We may find that it is the best course to support such a candidate for other reasons, but we must never allow people to be misled into confusing such religiosity with obedience to Christ.

On the other hand, if we find ourselves in disagreement with the extreme theocratic views held by some religionists which appear to erase the distinction between church and state, is the only option available that we retreat into the privatized irrelevance of a faith which remains quietly on the reservation and brings no prophetic word to the culture? Should we let our duty to accept the rights of other religions *in the civil sphere* be translated into a timidity about declaring what the Bible teaches concerning the uniqueness of the Christian faith, for fear of being branded moral McCarthyites? Can we as Christians rejoice with a candidate's claim that the supposed "wall of separation between church and state . . . has made us the most religious people on earth," when mere religion is as hopeless a course as outright paganism so far as the gospel of Jesus Christ is concerned? I think not.

It is true that in politics a candidate must attempt to build a unified constituency out of diverse groups, and thus he must try to lessen their differences and emphasize his similarities to all. The great temptation is for Christians to actually adopt this false image as reality. We may find that it is the best course to support such a candidate, for other reasons. But, as before, we must never allow people to be misled into confusing such religiosity with the gospel of God.

If I have outlined the competing positions in the current debate correctly, then the real danger should be apparent to those who have eyes to see. If we Christians allow ourselves to be forced to choose between these unbiblical alternatives, the opportunity provided by the new place currently being given to religion in public discourse will be lost. If we fail to speak clearly and boldly for Christ, the cutting edge of historic Christianity in our culture will be dulled, replaced by a generic American religion used by both parties for political advantage.

It is at this point that the Christian must take his stand because biblical Christianity declares that civil religion is idolatry and privatized faith is no faith at all. Both of these false options deny the truth of the Christian gospel—its unique character and its demand for the unrivaled lordship of Christ.

The danger is real. Enamored by the new power we appear to have in public life, Christians may succumb to the belief that a particular political program will usher in the kingdom of God. We would thus mute the more impolitic truths of the Christian message and trade our precious birthright, the eternal and unique gospel of Jesus Christ, for a mess of temporal political porridge. May God forbid!

And yet, though there is great temptation here, we cannot retreat from the political realm in order to safeguard the truth of the Christian faith. Christ himself will not permit it, and love for our neighbor cannot condone it. Why? Because it is Christ's teaching concerning his kingdom that so exposes the illusion of power of political kingdoms, and therein frees us from the idols which hold much of the world in bondage.

This is part of our Christian heritage that we must reclaim. Saint Augustine understood the nature of Christ's kingdom with great insight. When in 410 A.D. he was told that Rome had been sacked, he was deeply troubled. Yet he did not despair, for as he counseled his people: "All earthly cities are vulnerable. Men build them and men destroy them. At the same time there is the city of God which men did not build and cannot destroy and which is everlasting."

This knowledge destroys the political illusion that so insidiously infects Western culture. And, for want of the inoculation that this knowledge provides, Christians are catching the same disease. Its carriers are all around us.

In an evening newscast before the 1984 elections, I watched a parade of political candidates virtually promise to end the arms race, eliminate the deficit, settle the Middle East turmoil, and produce full employment. It was breathtaking.

Then I tried to remember—and couldn't—a single instance in which a candidate for any office, from city councilman to president, had ever admitted any problem that he or she could not solve once elected.

But in truth many problems cannot be cured—at least not the way the politicians promise. And even officials in the most powerful offices sometimes discover that they are not so powerful after all.

I remember one Friday afternoon in 1970 when President Nixon called me into his office. "I want an executive order creating a commission to study aid to nonpublic schools," he snapped. "Have it on my desk nine o'clock Monday morning." Mr. Nixon was frustrated that the creation of the commission, a campaign pledge, had been ignored by the Justice Department for eighteen months.

Simple enough, I thought. All I had to do was to find the right form, check it out with other staffers, and have it typed. Then bedlam broke loose. Another presidential assistant, John Erlichman, protested that I was "invading his area." The Attorney General was on the phone, as was the Commissioner of Education. Memos began flying back and forth as the bureaucracy suddenly came alive.

The battle that began that weekend went on for months. Eventually the order was issued, only to be soon forgotten.

This was no isolated instance. Career bureaucrats outlast presidents and are experts at stymieing orders they do not like. Many programs are deadlocked between Congress and the president; some agencies, after being launched with great fanfare, simply watch the problems they were created to solve steadily worsen.

Yet politicians of both parties continue to promise—and the electorate continues to expect—political solutions to all our ills. We go through the same cycle every election year. Why?

Two decades ago, Jacques Ellul, the eminent French historian, answered the question in a remarkably prophetic book, *The Political Illusion*. Ellul theorized that modern man increasingly turns to the state for answers to his problems even though the state cannot solve them. Politicians perpetuate the myth that it can since the illusion perpetuates their power; the media willingly collaborates since their coverage of government fuels their own power as well.

The result, Ellul wrote, is a "boundless growth" of the state, with an insatiable appetite for power; independent groups which involve people in meeting society's needs are the only way to lessen dependence on government and its eventual totalitarian control.

We Christians, of all people, should see through the

political illusion. We should understand that the real problems of our society are, at their root, moral and spiritual. Institutions and politicians are limited in what they can do, and we dare not confuse this limited good with the infinite good of the gospel. The kingdom of God will not arrive on Air Force One.

Certainly that is so in the criminal justice field. Crime is the result of wrong moral choices. Laws are needed to restrain evil, but penal institutions cannot deal with the ultimate problem: the human heart. That is why the gospel of Christ is the only real answer.

Even in foreign policy, governments are not all-powerful, as we are accustomed to think. The Marine presence in Lebanon was no deterrent to the centuries-old civil strife there. The British have learned the same lesson in Ulster.

Or take the example of Poland. Against the "powerful" array of Soviet divisions, thousands of school children have marched with their crucifixes held high, successfully resisting the communist government's edict to remove crosses from their classrooms. Where is the real power in Poland? Certainly not in the Politburo.

The political illusion poses three grave dangers:

First, as political solutions fail and problems worsen, people become cynical. In time, they became alienated from their own political process. We see this at both ends of the social spectrum. On the one hand, many of our poor disparage the political process, seeing no real hope for any change, and drop out of the system altogether. On the other hand, we see the growing indifference of the "yuppies," former political utopians now concerned for political good only as it contributes to private gain and personal comfort.

Second, the political illusion fosters a false security. Because the government is promising to deal with our problems, we do not have to bother. The government becomes our "brother's keeper," so we feel we are let off the hook.

Many of the government programs of the 1960's offer cases in point. As these social programs mushroomed, private welfare agencies declined. Because of the illusion that the government would take care of things, many individuals stopped caring for others.

As Alexander Solzhenitsyn charged at Harvard in 1978:

> We have placed too much hope in politics and social reforms, only to find out that we were being deprived of our most precious possession: our spiritual life. It is trampled by the party mob in the East, by the commercial one in the West. We are at a harsh spiritual crisis and a political impasse. All the celebrated technological achievements of progress . . . do not redeem the 20th century's moral poverty.

Political institutions provide no panaceas to the ills of our age, no matter how attractive they sound. They are surely no substitute for individual responsibility.

Third, and perhaps most dangerous, the political illusion suggests we must accumulate worldly power to advance the cause of Christ. But because that power can neither achieve utopia nor establish the ends of the gospel, another goal is soon substituted—power for its own sake.

I know about such things. Uniquely, perhaps, since I have worked both sides of the street. I have seen the White House transform young political idealists into prideful "supermen," myself included. The same thing can happen to the prestige-conscious businessman, the bullying shop steward, the domineering parent. For though worldly power is not inherently evil, its unbridled pursuit is powerfully corrupting. And we Christians are not exempt from its temptations.

When I worked in President Nixon's White House, one of my assignments was as a liaison with special-interest groups. For us, that included the religious.

From 1970 to 1972, I arranged special briefings in the

Roosevelt Room for religious leaders, ushered wide-eyed denominational leaders into the Oval Office for private sessions with the president, and even arranged dinner cruises on the presidential yacht for key leaders who just happened to come from states we had targeted in the 1972 election.

From these meetings grew very agreeable alliances. Religious leaders were able to make their points with the president—though most were so in awe they didn't. More important to us, we reaped handsome dividends on election day. The significance of Nixon's frequent photos with evangelical leaders was not lost on Bible-belt voters; and in the electoral-rich states of the Northeast, his open courting of the blue-collar Roman Catholic vote proved decisive.

I arm-twisted more than one religious leader into a partisan endorsement, and, on the whole, of all the groups I dealt with, I found religious leaders the most naive about politics. Maybe that is because so many come from sheltered backgrounds. Or perhaps it is the result of a mistaken perception of the demands of Christian charity: though Christian leaders understand abstract theological concepts about the depravity of man, which indeed includes politicians, they often want, perhaps with undue optimism, to see the best in them. Or, most worrisome of all, they may simply like to be around power.

It is easy to become enthralled with access to power. In time, however, without even knowing it, well-intentioned attempts to influence government policy can be so entangled with the politics of power that the clergy's primary goal becomes maintaining political access. When that happens, the gospel of Jesus Christ is held hostage to a political agenda—and religious leaders are little able to speak out and criticize it.

I cannot blame the politician when this happens. It is only natural that he will seek votes and electoral influence, just as Nixon and I did a decade ago, and as all politicians have done before and since. That is what politics is all about.

But the religious world must be on guard. Christians in

particular must heed our Lord's words: he who would lead, let him serve. That admonition is radically opposed to the self-aggrandizing nature of American politics. For the Christian, the goal in politics is not power, but justice.

The Old Testament prophets could serve as worthy models for today's leaders. They were political activists, angrily denouncing the abuse of privilege in places of power. But they were not much on invitations to the palace. Indeed, they fiercely guarded their independence, knowing they owed allegiance only to the King of all kings. This was true, too, of the early Christians; those who refused Caesar equal billing with God were fed to the lions.

But I am not at all confident that it is true today. There are all too many examples of religious leaders from both ends of the political spectrum sacrificing their integrity to the demands of political popularity. Christianity has survived persecution through the centuries, thrived on it in fact. But its leaders have never handled power very well.

By now, perhaps you are ready to throw up your hands in frustration. What on earth can a Christian do to be faithful to Christ in such a quagmire? Misled by red herrings concerning the supposed wall of separation between church and state, enticed by the false "friends" of civil religion and privatized faith, bewitched by the political illusion and seduced by the glamour of political power—we appear to be surrounded on every side by overwhelming odds.

At times like this I draw comfort, I am sorry to say, not from one of the spiritual giants of our time but from a crusty old Marine general under whom I served.

His name was Chesty Puller, and he was a legendary battlefield commander, one of the most decorated Marines ever, but also one of the most outspoken. The problem is that very little he said could ever be repeated in polite company.

Once when he was in command of the Marines in Korea, his units were nearly surrounded. Puller, who was always at the front lines, radioed back to the headquarters, "I have two regiments of North Koreans in front of me blocking the road." Moments later he radioed back, "The left flank has caved in and North Koreans are overrunning me there." Within minutes came another message, "The North Koreans have taken over the right flank." And finally he radioed the message, "They're behind me. It looks like an army behind me." But then came Puller's words, "They won't get away from me this time!"

And that is the way we Christians are to be in the world in which God has called us to live and work and serve him. So said the apostle Paul. We are to serve Christ in this difficult time in such a manner that, "the excellency of the power may be of God, and not of us. We are troubled on every side, yet not distressed; we are perplexed, but not in despair" (2 Cor 4:7-8; KJV).

And so in conclusion I would offer a few thoughts as to how the power of God in the gospel of Jesus Christ can be faithfully proclaimed in our political endeavors.

In the first place, we must make plain that the goal of our political involvement is neither a "religious establishment" nor an absolute wall of separation. These false options are dangerous both to the state and to the church. But at the same time we must boldly bear witness to the fact that, both now and in the past, Christian values brought to the democratic process are essential for a good and just social order.

This we must do not by simply wrapping our Bibles in the flag but by showing our brothers and sisters in Christ, on the one hand, that there are sound biblical reasons why we support the unique American experiment of separation of church and state. On the other hand, we must, with humility and reason, demonstrate to our friends in civil society who reject the Scriptures that our biblical concerns express the highest human values and bring to public policy principles wherein people may flourish.

In so doing, we must consistently be diligent to expose the political illusion. Each one of us must learn anew, if we had ever learned it before, to listen with healthy skepticism to the inflated rhetoric of the campaign trail. We need people ready to exercise what the underground grammarian Richard Mitchell has called "thoughtful discretion" when we listen to our foes, and yes, to our friends as well.

Last fall Assistant Press Secretary Larry Speakes gave us a first-rate example of the kind of sleight-of-tongue which so easily gives pseudosubstance to the political illusion. In the midst of campaign fervor he declared, "The president will not balance the budget on the backs of the American people."

Twenty years ago, "We won't balance the budget on the backs of the poor" was a popular rallying cry. Then it was the farm workers, minorities, the elderly. But now in one grand, magnanimous gesture, Speakes included everyone: "Not on the backs of the American people." *Newsweek* printed the statement as a serious campaign pledge. Network anchors repeated it without so much as a wry smile. But I ask you, on whose backs, then, will the budget be balanced? The French, perhaps?

Have we become so accustomed to absurdity that we accept it as the norm? For the Christian, refusing to do so helps to remind our brethren and inform the secular world that political institutions do not offer panaceas, no matter how attractive they may sound. We who know the Word and Truth recognize that the root of man's problem is spiritual: the only answer is Jesus Christ. Rather than be taken in by the political illusion, we ought to use it as a springboard for evangelism, proclaiming that Truth to the world.

Third, we Christians need to define our objectives carefully. Civil righteousness is a good end, and political power is an appropriate means to that end. But such power cannot bring in the kingdom or make people holy. For that end we must be careful to say boldly with Paul: "I am not ashamed of the gospel, because it is the power of God for the salvation of everyone who believes. . . . For in the gospel a righteousness from God is revealed, a righteousness that is by faith from first to last" (Rom 1:16-17).

As the late Christian thinker Francis Schaeffer argued, the objective for the Christian is modeled in the very nature of God. We seek justice, not power. Because of who God is, "Power is not first, but justice is first in society and law. The prince may have the power to . . . rule, but he does not have the right to do so without justice." This means that Christians who serve in the political sphere have a special obligation to a higher King. Such persons should heed Plato's words: "Only those who do not desire power are fit to hold it." This is radically opposed to the self-promoting nature of our political system. Yet it is the call of Jesus Christ. He teaches that to lead we must serve (Mt 20:25-28). Thus for the Christian, the call to political leadership is not a call to greater self-advancement but to greater death to self in service to others.

And in this service we must never confuse power with authority. Power is the ability to affect one's ends or purposes in the world; authority is having not only the might but also the right to do so. Power is often maintained by force alone; authority springs from a moral foundation.

True authority comes not from political power but from humble submission and obedience to the Word of God. Mother Teresa is the best living example. She spends her life in obedience to Christ, helping the powerless die with dignity; yet few people command more authority worldwide.

Fourth, we must be diligent to challenge and support our brothers and sisters in political office. All of us have the duty to bear one another's burdens; servants of the Lord in politics have a particularly heavy burden to bear.

Actually, we have a double obligation to those who so serve: we are enjoined by the word to pray for one another, and we are commanded to pray for "kings and all who are in authority." Let me assure you, from my own experience in politics, they need that in double measure.

Yet, to our lasting benefit, we have a great pantheon of heroes to guide us in political service. William Wilberforce is a great model for our times. Wilberforce was the Christian member of the British Parliament who led the twenty-year fight against the slave trade and ultimately won the abolition of slavery itself in England. I urge you to look to him, and other like him, as examples of what God may be pleased to do for a nation through the obedience of his servants.

Finally, one of the most powerful means we have at our disposal to affect political life is through the church; not by making our congregations political precincts, as we have both on the right and on the left in recent elections; rather by calling on the church to be the church.

In obedience to the lordship of Jesus Christ, we who follow him are called to be salt and light: salt rubbed into the meat as a preservative and light shining on a hill in the midst of self-imposed darkness.

When the church of Jesus Christ fulfills this high calling, we have the effect of preempting many of the problems that the state is eventually called on to solve. Secular politics simply cannot compete with the body of Christ, empowered by the Holy Spirit, in service.

That is why, in those nations where a godless rule attempts to eradicate Christianity, it is Christian service that is forbidden. In the Soviet Union, for example, Christians are free to worship, free to congregate in their church buildings. But these buildings, once glorious in their splendor, are now not much more than ornate museums. By law the Christians in the Soviet Union cannot have Christian schools, Christian service organizations, or work for public justice.

It has been this way since the beginning. In ancient Rome the pagan peoples were troubled and confused by the new sect. Not that they were against religion, for across the empire a bizarre diversity of religious expression was flourishing under the tolerant hand of the Roman masters. No, religion was thought of as an acceptable and important aspect of the culture. As long as Christians fit the mold and allowed themselves to be defined by the society, they were accepted.

But when the church began to express its unique calling,

refusing to be defined by popular images and proclaiming by word and deed that Christ is Lord, it came into open conflict with the world.

Thus it was from the beginning; and so it is today. Yet the early Christians had one great advantage over us; then it was clear that the surrounding culture was groping in the darkness of paganism, and thus it was clear that the culture should have no hand in defining the role of God's people in the world. But today we have grown accustomed to thinking of ourselves as a part of the "Christian West," living in a "Christian nation." That habit is hard to kick, for it has the narcotic effect of easing the painful reality of the stark contrast between twentieth century American culture and the calling of Christ to his church.

Yet we must kick that habit, if by serving heaven we are to be any earthly good. Our challenge is clear: we must reject the illusions, seductions, and false alternatives of the current political scene and reassert the ageless truth that Christ is Lord of lords, King of kings. With Athanasius, the great fourth century champion of the faith, we must stand for Christ *contra mundum*—"against the world."

In the very moment of our clearest opposition to the world, we will find that as witnesses to the Truth and Life we will have the inestimable privilege of helping to make his invisible kingdom visible in the world. For with Christ we will "preach the gospel to the poor . . . proclaim release to the captives, and recovery of sight to the blind; set free those who are downtrodden, and proclaim the favorable year of the Lord" (Lk 4:18-19).

# EIGHT

# Feminism, the Holy Trinity, and Language about God

*Deborah Malacky Belonick*

T HE LAST FEW YEARS have seen vast changes in many churches in liturgical rites and educational instruction in regard to proper language for God. The United Church of Christ, to give just one example, has published "Inclusive Language Guidelines" urging members to "avoid the use of masculine role names for God such as Lord, King, Father, Master, and Son," and instead to "use nonexclusive role names such as God, Creator, Sustainer, Mother/Father. Or use nonsex-specific words relating to the qualities of God such as Spirit, Holy One, Eternal One, Rock."[1] Feminist theologians chide those using the traditional terms as being sexist, ignorant of feminine images for God in Scripture, or unaware of the "oppressive patriarchal structure" which "invented" these terms for God.

A study of history shows that calling into question the language used for God is not a new pursuit. We must not think that we in the twentieth century are the only ones who ever wrestled with the traditional doxology for God: "Father, Son,

*117*

and Holy Spirit." The ways that the issue has been raised, and the ways Christians in the past have responded to it, have much to teach us today as we seek to respond to accusations by feminist theologians that patriarchalism and human imagination are responsible for the traditional trinitarian terms for God.

There is a tendency among contemporary Christians to ignore any history between the time of St. Paul's salvific experience with God and our own. This tendency produces a gap of twenty centuries. We have a company of saints who have gone before us as great clouds of witnesses (Heb 12:1), yet there is a lack of awareness of their situations, an ignorance of their struggles. This historical unawareness is distressing, particularly in discussions of feminist theology and language about God, because in this regard sisters and brothers of the past have much to teach us. Specifically, Christians of the fourth century have much to teach us.

The fourth century was the period of the all-consuming questions: who and what is Jesus Christ? His humanity, divinity, person, and nature were the topics of great debates, which examined his relationship to humanity as well as to the other members of the Trinity. During these fourth century debates, the traditional doxology for God—"Father, Son, and Holy Spirit"—was also challenged and debated.

A study of the Christian controversies of the fourth century leads to two important conclusions. First, the terms "Father, Son, and Holy Spirit" have a precise theological meaning which is not communicated by any other terms for God. Second, the traditional doxology did not emerge as a reflection of patriarchal culture.

On the first point, two fourth century theologians who were embroiled in controversies over the proper terms for God, Athanasius and Gregory of Nyssa, are especially worthwhile for our study.

Athanasius was defending the traditional trinitarian names against the Arians, a group which preferred to call the first person of the Trinity "Creator" rather than "Father." Arians claimed that Jesus Christ was not the Son of God but merely a superior creature; therefore, "Father" was a fleshly, foolish, improper term for God. In reply to the Arians, Athanasius tried to explain the importance of the biblical divine names, "Father, Son, and Holy Spirit."

Using a term such as "Creator," said Athanasius, makes God dependent on creatures for his identity, even his existence. If creation did not exist, he asked, would this Creator-God cease to be? If creation had never existed, what would be the proper term for God?

In addition, Athanasius argued, the word "Creator" could be used to describe *any* of the members of the Trinity. It would be wrong to refer to the Father alone as Creator because the Bible states:

> In the beginning God created the heavens and the earth. The earth was without form and void, and darkness was upon the face of the deep; and the *Spirit of God* was moving over the face of the waters. (Gen 1:1-2)

> In the beginning was the Word, and the Word was with God, and the Word was God. He was in the beginning with God; *all things were made through him,* and without him was not anything made that was made. (Jn 1:1-3)

According to Scripture, the Trinity acts in concert. They all create; they all save (Jn 5:21; Acts 2:24; Rom 1:4); they all sanctify (Eph 5:26; 1 Thes 5:23).

Athanasius argued that the names of God had to describe more than God's action toward creation. "There are, as it were, two different sets of names which may be used for God," explained Athanasius. "One set (Creator, Savior, Sanctifier) refers to God's deeds or acts, that is, to his will and counsel. The other set (Father, Son, Holy Spirit) refers to God's own essence and being."[2] Athanasius insisted that these two sets should be formally and consistently distinguished.

In Athanasius' view, we should use the terms "Father, Son, and Holy Spirit" when speaking about the existence of God as three persons in a community of love, when speaking about the relationships among members of the Trinity without regard to their economic acts toward creation. "God's 'being,'" Athanasius reasoned, "has absolute ontological priority over God's action and will: God is much more than just 'Creator.' When we call God 'Father,' we mean something higher than his relation to creatures."[3]

Gregory of Nyssa faced similar problems when dealing with a sect known as the Eunomians, who believed that Christ was unlike God the Father by nature and was instead a "created energy." For this reason, Eunomians refused to call God "Father." In response, Gregory sought to explain the character of the Holy Trinity, the relationships among the persons of the Trinity, and the church's insistence on the traditional terms, "Father, Son, and Holy Spirit."

First, said Gregory, there was no more adequate theologian than the Lord himself, who without compulsion or mistake designated the Godhead "Father, Son, and Holy Spirit" (Mt 28:19).[4]

Further, Gregory said, these names are not indications that God is a male or a man, for God transcends human gender.[5] Gregory insisted that the division of humanity into male and female had "no relation to the divine Archetype."[6] Rather, the names "Father, Son, and Holy Spirit" imply *relationships* among the persons of the Trinity, and distinguish them as separate *persons* who exist in a community of love. The names lead us to contemplate the *correct* relationships among the three persons; they are clues to the inner life of the Trinity.

Gregory wrote:

> While there are many other names by which the deity is indicated in the historical books of the Bible, in the prophets, and in the law, our master Christ passes by all

these and commits to us these titles as better able to bring us to the faith about the Self-Existent, declaring that it suffices for us to cling to the titles 'Father, Son, and Holy Spirit' in order to attain to the apprehension of him who is absolutely Existent, who is one and yet not one.[7]

Gregory states that it is with the terms "Father, Son, and Holy Spirit" that women and men can enter into the depths of God's life, somewhat equipped to understand the inner relationships and persons of the Trinity.

Of particular interest in our own day is Gregory's explanation of the term "Father," which is under scrutiny by feminist theologians as a harmful metaphor that resulted from a patriarchal church structure and culture.

The name "Father," said Gregory, leads us to contemplate (1) a Being who is the source and cause of all and (2) the fact that this Being has a relationship with another person—one can only be "Father" if there is a child involved.[8] Thus, the human term "Father" leads one naturally to think of another member of the Trinity, to contemplate more than is suggested by a term such as "Creator" or "Maker." By calling God "Father," Gregory notes, one understands that there exists with God a Child from all eternity, a second person who rules with him, is equal and eternal with him.[9]

"Father" also connotes the initiator of a generation, the one who begets life rather than conceiving it and bringing it to fruition in birth.[10] This is the mode of existence, the way of origin and being, of the first person of the Trinity. He acts in trinitarian life in a mode of existence akin to that of a father in the earthly realm. Before time, within the mystery of the Holy Trinity, God generated another person, the Son, as human fathers generate seed.

Nowhere does Gregory suggest that this "Father" is a male creature: "It is clear that this metaphor contains a deeper meaning than the obvious one," he notes.[11] The deeper meaning is found in a passage of Paul to the Ephesians: "For this reason I bow my knees before the Father, from whom every family ( πατριά , fatherhood) in heaven and on earth is named"(Eph 3:14-15). This passage implies that God is the one, true, divine Father, whose generative function human fathers imitate in a creaturely, imperfect way. When God generates a Child, the generation is eternal, and transcends time and space, unlike human fathers, who imitate this generative function but are bound in time, space, and creaturely "passions" as Gregory notes.[12]

All the patristic writers insist that God is not male, but God possesses a generative characteristic for which the best analogy in the human realm is that of a human father generating seed. Hence, the word "Father" for God is the human word most adequate to describe the first person of the Holy Trinity, who possesses this unique characteristic.

This divine Father is as different from earthly fathers as the divine is from the human.[13] Nevertheless, it is *fatherhood* and not *motherhood* which describes his mode of life, his relationship to the second person of the Trinity, and even his personal characteristics. The first person of the Trinity does not just *act* like a father (though he sometimes acts like a mother!). Rather, he *possesses* divine fatherhood in a perfect way. That God's fatherhood transcends and is the perfection of human fatherhood is part of the meaning of Jesus' statement in Matthew 23:9: "And call no man your father on earth, for you have one Father, who is in heaven."

Clement of Alexandria, another fourth century Christian teacher, expressed this idea most aptly: "God is himself love, and because of his love, he pursued us. [In the eternal generation of the Son] the ineffable *nature* of God is father; in his sympathy *with us* he is mother."[14]

In his explanation of the term "Son," which is also a term often considered noninclusive in our era, Gregory of Nyssa reiterates that this also is a precise theological term leading one to the inner relationships of the Godhead. It has primacy over other scriptural terms. He says:

While the names which Scripture applies to the Only-begotten are many, we assert that none of the other names is closely connected with reference to him that begot him. For we do not employ the name "Rock" or "Resurrection" or "Shepherd" or "Light" or any of the rest, as we do the name "Son of the Father," with a reference to the God of all. It is possible to make a twofold division of the signification of the divine names, as it were by a scientific rule: for to one class belongs the indication of his lofty and unspeakable glory; the other class indicates the variety of providential dispensation.[15]

All sorts of epithets for God are available to humanity through revelation—goodness, love, mother, fire. But none of these are exchangeable or comparable to the revelation of God as Father, Son, and Holy Spirit. These are the terms by which humanity enters trinitarian life to discover the unique persons of the Trinity and their distinguishable marks.

The traditional trinitarian terms are precise theological terms, not easily exchangeable for any others. They lead us to the persons of the Trinity as well as define relationships between them. To be unbegotten, begotten, and in procession are characteristics of the persons of the Father, Son, and Holy Spirit. Paternity, generation, and procession are the unique marks of the respective persons.

In Western theology it has become common to say that the persons of the Trinity are defined by these relations, as Thomas Aquinas wrote, *"Persona est relatio."*[16] But in the Eastern church, the persons were prior to the relationship, the persons *possessed* the characteristics of paternity, generation, and procession. These were their personal ("hypostatic") characteristics, some truths known about their persons.[17]

Although Scripture mentions many metaphors for God—rock (Ps 18:2, 31, 46); shepherd (Jn 10:11); savior, mother (Is 66:13)—the personal names "Father, Son, and Holy Spirit" were not to be considered in the same category with them.[18]

They were in a category superior to all other names, and, when human imagination about God was negated and exhausted, there emerged the personal names, "Father, Son, and Holy Spirit."[19]

What about the feminist allegation that the traditional doxology is the product of a patriarchal structure, of a "male" theology? Did the patristic writers harbor animosity toward women or femininity? Did they use masculine terms for God, the source of all life, because they mistakenly thought that human fathers are the sole source of human life? Indeed, the opposite appears to be true.

First, some women did have opportunities to express their understanding of the Godhead. Macrina, elder sister of two of the greatest theologians of the fourth century, Basil the Great and the aforementioned Gregory of Nyssa, was referred to by her brothers as the "teacher."[20] It was she who raised them in the faith and instructed them in the theology of the Father, Son, and Holy Spirit. She defended these titles as revelations recorded in Scripture.[21]

Likewise, Nina, the evangelizer of the Georgians, converted that entire nation by her teaching of Jesus Christ and of the Holy Trinity—Father, Son, and Holy Spirit.[22] She did so of her own volition: she was not commissioned by the bishops.

Second, the most accurate way to describe the church fathers' attitude toward women would be not animosity but ambivalence.[23] One can indeed find passages in their writings deriding women for their weak wills and for leading the human race into sin (John Chrysostom writes that "the woman taught once and ruined all"[24]). But one also finds passages extolling women for being of great character and teaching the gospel better than men. Gregory of Nazianzen, in writing of his parents, explains that his father's virtue was "the result of his wife's prayers and guidance, and it was from her that he learned his ideal of a good shepherd's life.... They [his parents] have been rightly assigned, each to either sex; he is the ornament of men, she of women, and not only the ornament, but the pattern of virtue."[25]

Jerome says his readers may laugh at him for so often "dwelling on the praises of mere women . . . [but] we judge of people's virtue not by their sex but by their character, and hold those to be of the highest glory who have renounced both rank and wealth."[26]

It must also be noted that in several instances the church was much fairer toward women than the surrounding culture. Gregory of Nazianzen, the great trinitarian theologian, exemplified this by upbraiding the men of his flock in regard to a civil law which meted out strict punishment for wives committing adultery but disregarded husbands committing the same crime:

> [Let me discuss] chastity, in respect of which I see that the majority of men are ill-disposed, and that their laws are unequal and irregular. For what was the reason why they restrained the woman but indulged the man, and why a woman who practices evil against her husband's bed is an adulteress (and the legal penalties for this are very severe), but if a husband commits fornication against his wife, he has no account to give? I do not accept this legislation; I do not approve this custom. Those who made the law were men, and therefore the legislation is hard on women.[27]

Fourth, it appears that it was not unknown to the leaders of the fourth century church that mothers as well as fathers contributed as sources to the making of a child. John Chrysostom wrote:

> A man leaving *them* that begat him, and from whom he was born, is knit to his wife. And then the one flesh is, father, and mother, and the child *from the substance of the two* commingled. For indeed, by the commingling of *their* seeds the child is produced."[28]

Yet, even with this knowledge of mothers and fathers both acting as sources in the life process, the Church insisted on using the exclusive term "Father" for God.

Perhaps even more interesting, patristic writers never excluded the ideas that women were made in the image of God or that human femininity had some relationship to God. In many texts there appears the idea that women, with their femininity, are closely associated with the person of the Holy Spirit, and the Spirit's mode of life.[29] In the patristic period, the church fathers compared the procession of the Holy Spirit from the Father with the procession of Eve from Adam.[30]

Later, in the seventh century, Anastasius of Sinai wrote: "Eve, who proceeded from Adam, signifies the proceeding hypostasis of the Holy Spirit. This is why God did not breathe in her the breath of life; she was already the type of the breathing and life of the Holy Spirit."[31] Especially in Syriac hymnody, the association between human femininity and the mode of existence of the Holy Spirit was stressed.[32] Therefore, the "masculine" terms used in the trinitarian names are not the result of disdain for the feminine.

With this evidence, it is clear that the patristic writers were interested in preserving the scriptural terms of "Father, Son, and Holy Spirit" as revelations from God, rather than as reflections of patriarchal culture. This is evident from their frequent appeals to Scripture for the bases of their arguments.[33] These terms are precise theological terms, keys for understanding the Trinity, and are not interchangeable with such feminist formulas as "Mother, Daughter, Holy Spirit," nor even with other attributes and activities of God such as "Creator, Savior, and Sanctifier." They have been revealed to humanity to serve as the most adequate language available to describe the three members of the Trinity. They are revelations from God that help us enter the Trinitarian abyss and to meet the one true God.

In view of this historical background, it appears the arguments supporting "nonexclusive" language changes for

God are untenable—incompatible with Scripture, apostolic teachings, and Christian experience. Against the historical backdrop of church life, the terms "Father, Son, and Holy Spirit" appear not as exchangeable metaphors, human imaginings, or pillars of a patriarchal culture, but rather as precise terms revealed by Jesus Christ through the Holy Spirit and preserved in the canon of Scripture.

The challenge to Christians today compares to the challenge to Christians in the fourth century: to preserve these names as gifts from God which give us clues to his inner life, for us as adopted children through his Son, Jesus Christ, our Lord.

# Notes

*All *NPNF* notations refer to *A Select Library of Nicene and Post Nicene Fathers of the Christian Church,* Schaff, Philip, D.D., L.L.D., and Wace, Henry D.D., eds. (Grand Rapids, Michigan: Wm B. Eerdmans Publishing Co.). All *PG* notations refer to *Patrologia graeca,* Migne, Paris, 1878-96.

1. "Inclusive Language Guidelines for Use and Study in the United Church of Christ" (Church Leadership Resources, P.O. Box 179, St. Louis, MO 63166, June 1980), p. 5.

2. Georges Florovsky, *Aspects of Church History: Volume Four in the Collected Works of Georges Florovsky* (Belmont, Mass.: Nordland Publishing Company, 1975), p. 52.

3. *Against the Arians, PG* 26:80A-81A; *NPNF* 1:33.

4. *Against Eunomius, PG* 45:505A-516B; *NPNF* 2:2.

5. Gregory of Nazianzen, fourth century, also notes that the names of God have nothing whatever to do with human gender categories. (*Fifth Theological Oration, NPNF* 7.)

6. *On the Making of Man, NPNF* 16:14.

7. *Against Eunomius, PG* 45:469A; *NPNF* 2:2.

8. *Against Eunomius, PG* 45:469B-D; *NPNF* 2:9.

9. *Against Eunomius, PG* 45:617A-628B; *NPNF* 4:1.

10. Feminist theologians argue that woman, as well as man, is the source of

all life, and therefore this first person of the Holy Trinity may be called "Mother" as well as "Father." The early Church was well aware that both male and female cells were required to create life, and that male was not the only source of life (John Chrysostom, *Homily XX on Ephesians 5:31*). The Church, however, always maintained a distinction between begetting and bearing, between the male and female contributions and modes of action in creating life. The male cell is the generator, inaugurator and impregnator; there are distinctions in the basic biological act of procreation.

11. *Against Eunomius, NPNF* 1:23.

12. *Against Eunomius, NPNF* 4:1.

13. *Against Eunomius, PG* 45:444A-B; *NPNF* 1:39.

14. *Quis Dives Salvetur? PG* 9.641C.

15. *Against Eunomius, NPNF* 3:7.

16. *Summa Theologica,* Ia, q. 29, 9.4.

17. Vladimir Lossky, *The Mystical Theology of the Eastern Church* (Crestwood, N.Y.: St. Vladimir Seminary Press, 1976) pp. 57-58. Also, "The Procession of the Holy Spirit," in Lossky, *The Image and Likeness of God* (Crestwood, N.Y.: St. Vladimir Seminary Press, 1974). Each person (hypostasis) of the Godhead possesses a, τρόπος ὑπάρξεως , *i.e.*, *mode of existence,* which is a characteristic of the person. Western theologians, typically fearful of tritheism, tend toward a unitarian position of saying there exists one God in three modes of existence; rather than contending as do the Orthodox fathers that God exists in three persons who each are marked by and *possess* a particular mode of existence.

18. In modern usage, the word "metaphor" indicates the juxtaposing of two dissimilar objects, in which one thing is likened to another as if it were the other: "The child is a beautiful flower." Patristic writers, however, did not view metaphors in this limited sense. Descriptions of God were "metaphorical" only in that they could not express exactly the full reality of the Divinity. In addition, the term "Father" was not on the same level as other "metaphors." Gregory of Nyssa states: ". . . metaphors innumerable are taken from human life to illustrate symbolically divine things (*e.g.,* hand, eye, eyelids, hearing, heart). As, then, each of these names has a human sound, but not a human meaning, so also that of Father, while applying equally to life divine and human, hides a distinction between the uttered meanings exactly proportionate to the difference existing between the subjects of this title . . . there may be, so far as words go, some likeness between man and the Eternal, yet the gulf between these two worlds is the real measure of the separation of meanings." (*Against Eunomius* Book I:39 in *NPNF*) Here, Gregory is not comparing two dissimilar objects, but a similar characteristic (in this case, fatherhood) shared by two objects, and separated only by the "gulf" between human and divine. This is a true *carry-over* (in Greek, a μετά - φέρω ) of a quality from the Divine to the human.

19. The fact that a personal God arises out of the "apophatic" methodology,

that one meets God face to face after casting aside all human delusion, is stressed in all of the fathers and mystics of the Church. Lossky, *Orthodox Theology* (Crestwood, N.Y.: St. Vladimir Seminary Press, 1978), p. 32ff. It is an Orthodox dogma that God remains unknowable in "essence," that abyss of Divinity which forever is transcendent and unknowable. What is revealed to humanity are God's "energies" (in Western terms, "attributes"). God bursts forth from hiding to communicate with human beings, to reveal something of the Deity. Pseudo-Dionysius authored works on both "cataphatic" (*Divine Names* and two lost treatises, *Symbolic Theology* and *On Hypotyposes* or *Outlines of Theology*) and "apophatic" (*Mystical Theology*) methodology in the fifth century. His "two ways" were explained more fully in the fourteenth century by St. Gregory Palamas, according to Lossky, *In the Image and Likeness of God*, p. 23 *passim*.

20. "On the Soul and the Resurrection," as found in *NPNF*, Volume V, Schaff, Philip, D.D., L.L.D. and Wace, Henry, D.D., eds., (Grand Rapids, Michigan: Wm B. Eerdmans Publishing Co., 1982) p. 430ff.
21. *Ibid.* p. 439.
22. *The Life of St. Nina, Equal of the Apostles and Enlightener of Georgia* (with a service to her life included) (Jordanville, N.Y.: Holy Trinity Russian Orthodox Monastery, 1977).
23. Elizabeth Clark, *Women in the Early Church* (Wilmington, Delaware: Michael Glazier, Inc., 1983), p. 15.
24. *Homily IX, On Timothy 2:11-15.*
25. *Funeral Oration on His Sister Gorgonia, NPNF* 5.
26. *Letter CXXVII, To Principia, NPNF* 5.
27. *On the Words of the Gospel: Homily 37:6, on Matthew 19:1-12, PG* 36:289A-B; *NPNF* 6.
28. *Homily XX, On the Letter to the Ephesians 5:31, PG* 62:139-140.
29. John Meyendorff, *Catholicity and the Church* (Crestwood, N.Y.: St. Vladimir Seminary Press, 1983), p. 24.
30. Lossky, *Orthodox Theology*, pp. 69-70.
31. *On the Image and Likeness; PG* 89, col. 1145BC.
32. Joan Schaupp, *Woman: Image of the Holy Spirit* (Denville, N.J.: Dimension Books, 1975), pp. 89-91.
33. For example, see Gregory of Nyssa, *Against Eunomius, NPNF* 2:1, 2.

# NINE

# Christian Advance or Retreat? Sorting the Indicators in American Society

*Steve Clark*

THERE ARE TWO WAYS we can see the importance of the topic, "Christian Advance or Retreat," for this conference. First, many of us seem to have a concern with the various political and social movements in American society. If that is our concern, then where things are going in terms of the advance or decline of Christianity in the country is very significant. As the experience of the Christian Democratic parties in Europe and Latin America shows, one can mount a Christian effort in the political and social sphere and see some very significant gains in different areas. But if the Christian commitment of the people gets eroded, sooner or later one's political endeavors get eroded as well. If one does not keep an eye on one's base of support, sooner or later one may be in trouble, even if one currently seems to be making great gains politically.

The second perspective yields a similar result. Many of us

here are especially concerned with the pastoral dimension of church life, with how to care for God's people. If these people are being undermined in their Christian commitment, that is important to know. At the same time, if there are some good currents that can lead to ways of making gains, that is good to know, too. It is worth trying to be sensitive to what is happening in the overall social environment that may affect pastoral interests.

As the title of this presentation suggests, there are two opinions around. One is the opinion that Christianity is advancing, the other that it is retreating in the United States today. I am going to begin by considering the opinion that Christianity is making a great advance in the United States today.

I see two groups of people holding a Christian advance view. One is the group that experiences what I would call "Gallup Poll Euphoria." I do not mean that in a deprecating sense. In recent years there have been polls indicating certain advances for the Christian people, and some observers have taken heart from them. I think there is a mood among a number of people that is rooted in whole or in part in those polls.

Gallup Poll Euphoria, as near as I can see, is likewise related to membership in successful, conservative Christian churches and groups. As I think we all know, there are a number of Christian churches and groups in the United States that have been steadily growing in the last twenty years, and some that have been steadily declining. Many of the people who hold strong Christian advance opinions come from the groups that are growing. Another factor that feeds the Gallup Poll Euphoria is a positive-thinking orientation. One believes that one is supposed to have a positive, faith-filled thinking and therefore ought to think in terms of Christian advance.

Finally, one last source of Gallup Poll Euphoria is a Reagan-era conservative optimism. Many of those who have been most heartened by the poll results also are taking heart from what they see as conservative advances in general in the country.

This summary of factors is a bit impressionistic, but I think that these attitudes tend to cluster together in a recognizable grouping of people and produce a certain optimistic orientation toward Christian advance.

There is, however, another group holding the Christian advance view—those who are reacting to the myth of progressive secularization. They hold that there is a strong and, in fact, growing Christian presence in American society. The following observation, quoted from a good article by Richard John Neuhaus, in the *Christian Legal Society Quarterly,* expresses this viewpoint well:

> In recent years, massive survey research has demonstrated that Americans are probably more religious than at any time in our history, and that their professed values are overwhelmingly grounded in the Judeo-Christian tradition. The proposition that America is inevitably becoming a more secular society—a proposition that has assumed dogmatic status in our communications media, textbooks, and courts—is not supported by the evidence. The radical secularization of law does not result from the absence of shared moral vision among the American people but from the exclusion of that vision in legal deliberation.[1]

I believe there is something to that opinion, but I think it is seriously overstated.

The dictum that one should be careful not to believe one's own propaganda has a helpful application in this context. There is a core of truth in the reaction against the myth of progressive secularization, and when one thinks about communicating on the subject, there is a lot to be said for stressing the fact that the United States is not simply becoming progressively secularized. A little rhetoric is not out of order in making a point in an environment that tends to be prejudiced against it. On the other hand, when Christians are taking stock of their actual situation, when we are asking the question

"What do we have to do to succeed?", then we have to be more careful. If everything is flowing along from glory to glory, we do not have to do anything to succeed. If we are misled, by some of the things we ourselves say in a different context, into taking an excessively positive view, then we could be in serious trouble.

Let us look at the Christian advance view closely. What reason do we have for believing there is a Christian advance in the United States? I will begin by examining some positive factors that have come out of the various surveys and other research.

First of all, a very high percentage of people in the United States say that they believe in God; one poll reports 94 percent. That puts the United States second only to India among the major nations in the world. We would probably want to ask questions about what kind of God they believe in in India. Indeed we may also want to raise questions about what exactly the Americans in their polls mean by belief in God. But nevertheless, even allowing for serious theological vagueness in the survey questions and in the minds of those polled, the fact that 94 percent of Americans are willing to say they believe in God is significant.

Second, a large number of Americans attend church or synagogue every weekend: a little over 40 percent. Compared to the rest of the Western world, that figure is very high. Significantly, there has been a 5 percent rise in church or synagogue attendance among college students since 1975, although still less than 40 percent of them attend in an average week.

Finally, there has been a significant rise in interest in religion and religious activities over the last five years. Moreover, the increase of interest in Bible studies is particularly prominent.

These are all positive factors. To them I would like to add another, one that is not usually mentioned in polls but that I consider even more significant: the vitality of the conservative, more doctrinally-orthodox churches and groups, Catholic and Protestant alike. It is the fundamentalists and conservative evangelicals that are growing the most. Likewise, and probably relatedly, the missionary movement in the United States is quite impressive, as is the growing Christian school movement.

Putting all that together, we would have to say that there are genuine indicators of a Christian advance. I draw the conclusion that we are in a good time for evangelistic outreach, for growing and moving forward. There is religious interest; there is a great deal of receptiveness to Christianity. We are not just scratching stony soil.

There is, however, a negative side to the positive evidence. The long-term trends are less reassuring than the short-term trends. Church attendance is considerably lower than it was thirty years ago—10 percent lower than it was thirty years ago, even with the small recent rise. In addition, some important indicators of the role of religious activities in American society show a decline over a forty year period; for example, the percentage of books published which are religious in nature, and the percentage of the gross national product which is donated to religious charities. Moreover, people in their twenties are *less* likely to attend church than people over fifty, whereas twenty-five years ago they were *more* likely to attend church than people in their fifties—a remarkable reverse in interest in church activities in young people relative to older people. We can reasonably expect that older people will graduate sooner from this life and, therefore, the higher percentage of religious activities among them indicates which way the long-term trend is going. (For a recent discussion of these trends, I would refer you to an article by Patrick Egan, "Is America Becoming More Christian or Less?" in *Pastoral Renewal,* March 1984.)

Other sources present data regarding the context of Americans' religious beliefs which is also worth paying attention to. The recent and noteworthy *Middletown III* survey of Muncie,

Indiana, shows a rise in church attendance, and the report as a whole gives a positive view of the state of religion in Muncie.[2] However, less prominent in the report are some interesting facts about Muncians' religious views which have some bearing on how we interpret the religious situation. For example, in 1924, 94 percent of the high school students responded affirmatively to the statement, "Christianity is the one true religion, and all people should be converted to it." But only 41 percent responded affirmatively in 1977. I personally would not have wanted the question to be put that way. One of the troubles with surveys of religion is that they often do not ask the right questions or ask them in the best way. Nonetheless, the response gives us a general indication that convictions about the importance of Christianity and of missionary and evangelistic outreach have declined, even though church attendance and other "Christian" indicators have gone up. Another example of paradoxical shifts of beliefs and practices concerns the Bible. While one poll shows a 5 percent rise between 1944 and the present in those who read the Bible, and a rise in participation in Bible study groups, the same poll shows a decline of 10 percent in those who believe that the Bible is the word of God. Again, there was an activity rise but a content decline. The conclusion I would draw from these kinds of statistics is that a rise in religious interest or activity is not necessarily a rise in orthodox, evangelical Christianity. That does not mean that there is no type of Christian advance going on, but it does help us to be more accurate about the type of Christian advance that we see.

Now I would like to present the Christian retreat view. Fifteen years ago, in a study of secularization in English society, Bryan Wilson, a sociologist, noted how thorough was the decline of Christianity in that country and compared it to the case of the United States, where the pattern of Christian church attendance and Christian activities has been quite different. He wrote:

Superficially then, and in contrast to evidence from Europe and particularly from Protestant Europe, the United States manifests a high degree of religious activity. And yet, on this evidence, no one is prepared to suggest that America is other than a secularized country.[3]

As an indicator of that, Wilson went on to discuss the values that shape American life and what happens in American daily living. In doing so he put his finger on what we most need to pay attention to in assessing Christian retreat. What indeed is happening on the "values and way of life" front?

Let me begin with an example that is clear-cut, well documented and uncontroversial—what people call the sexual revolution. There has been, in recent years in American society, a massive change in attitude and in practice with regard to premarital sex. Numerous surveys indicate a steady rise in premarital sexual activity among adolescents and young adults even in sectors of American society that had previously been most resistant. (Another article in *Pastoral Renewal*, "A Revolution in Premarital Sex," June 1982, summarizes research findings from 1958 to 1981.) Studies of youth in every region of the country and in various educational and economic groups consistently revealed increases—often very large increases—in what Christians used to call "fornication." According to the Census Bureau, the decade of the 1970s showed a 300 percent rise in the number of unmarried people living together, to a total of 2,000,000. Christians still lag behind the secular trend, but they are catching up. For instance, 62 percent of teens thirteen to eighteen years of age polled by Gallup in 1981 thought premarital sex was not wrong (71 percent of the boys sixteen to eighteen). Among the regular churchgoers, boys and girls thirteen to eighteen years, it was 52 percent. An especially striking change is seen among Catholics. In 1963, a National Opinion Research Center Poll showed that 70 percent of Catholics in their twenties believed premarital sex was wrong. In 1979, only 17 percent thought that. A recent survey by the Search Institute of Minneapolis of intact churchgoing families, mostly middle-class Protestants in the Midwest, shows one fourth of the ninth-grade boys as having engaged in sexual intercourse.[4] That is extraordinary. Ninth grade is quite early, and the fact that very few of the parents are or have been divorced is an indication that we are dealing with the elite of Christian families.

What does all this mean? It means that if you have a Christian youth group in your church or fellowship, many, perhaps most, of the young people in your group have probably engaged in what those of us who accept the scriptural teaching would consider very serious immorality.

In other words, at the same time that there are some positive indicators of religious activity, there is also a very serious decline in terms of the Christian way of life.

My experience indicates that most churches and Christian groups—and most Christian parents—do not realize how serious this decline is. They see their church-attending youth as "good kids." They often do not know what is going on in their own household because the young people are, in many ways, doing well on a variety of counts.

I just had a discussion with one of the youth team workers here in our community. We were talking about some of the things that were going on with some of the young people. I asked if he thought that the parents knew anything about what he told me was going on. He answered by telling of a conversation he had had with one girl in which she said very clearly, "I wouldn't think of telling my parents I've done these things. They think I'm a good kid." I think that is fairly typical of what is going on. There often is a big difference between what parents and pastoral leaders think is happening and what objective sociological surveys show. Without necessarily leaving the churches or abandoning religious activities, Christian young people have been quietly joining the American sexual revolution.

Two observations may be made here. The first is that American society is becoming less accepting of Christian values and behavior. Many people in American society would say, "Let Christians believe what they want in private." We Christians in the United States, in fact, do not experience much conflict over our personal beliefs. On the other hand, there is real warfare regarding our way of life. The predominant message to Christians in many secular institutions is: "Change your way of life because we are making a new society with a new set of values." One of the values many secular people are building into that new society is the elimination of restrictive sexual morality.

The second observation is that when American society changes, American Christians change with it. They may change more slowly than the secular mainstream, but they do adopt the secular values and behavior patterns. That is the dark side of what the surveys and polls show us. The Christian way of life, as a distinctive approach based on the truths of revelation and the Christian worldview, is being eroded at the same time as religious activities seem to be holding reasonably steady or even, as in the last few years, increasing slightly.

The divorce picture tends to corroborate this view. As we know, divorce today is at a tremendously high level. In fact, the divorce rate has been rising ever since the Civil War. From 1860 to the end of the nineteenth century, the divorce rate more than tripled (from 1.2 to 4.0 divorces per 1,000 marriages). Then from the turn of the century to 1950, the divorce rate more than doubled (from 4.0 to 10.2 divorces per 1,000 marriages). In the most recent period, the divorce rate has doubled again (from 2.5 divorces per 1,000 population in 1950 to 5.2 in 1980). In the 1980s the rate has plateaued at a level more than twelve times as high as it was 120 years ago.[5]

And here, as in the case of premarital sex, Christians are

following the trend. One-third of American adults who identify themselves as Protestants have been divorced.[6] Ten million Americans who identify themselves as "born-again Christians" have been divorced.[7] Of course, among those who call themselves Protestants or born again are many people with little connection with any church. But even so, the figures are significant of what is going on among Christians in our society. When it comes to Catholics, in particular:

> From 1972-73 to 1982-83 the proportion [of Catholics who have been divorced or legally separated] has risen from one in every seven Catholics ever married to one in every four. While the percentage of those ever married who have been divorced and separated in the general population rose by 50 percent in the ten-year period, the percentage of the divorced and separated among Catholics rose by 90 percent. As a result the percentage of the divorced and separated among Catholics ever married is higher today than was the percentage of divorced and separated in United States society as a whole a decade ago.[8]

In other words, where the Catholics used to be able to maintain a somewhat distinctive way of life in overall culture, now they are catching up to the secular trend. They are now even at a worse place than American society was only ten years ago.

Christians' adoption of non-Christian patterns of behavior regarding premarital sex and divorce is not an isolated phenomenon. Attitudes toward sex are related to many other aspects of life—one's willingness to subordinate one's desires to the common good, one's vision of self-fulfillment and success, one's willingness to submit to the authority of God's word. Furthermore, other studies of Christians' attitudes and practices confirm the picture of Christians following secular trends that conflict with Christian values. To give a recent example, two researchers who have a fairly conservative

Protestant theological point of view, George Barna and William Paul McKay, report survey results showing American Christians' worldly approach to life. I emphasize their theological conservatism because it means that they use the term "Christian" in a much more restrictive way than many other pollsters. Among their findings:

> A recent national survey discovered that no fewer than seven of ten Christians are prone to hedonistic attitudes about life.[9]

By this they mean attitudes such as "an individual is free to do whatever pleases him as long as it does not hurt others," "pain or suffering cannot be the means of becoming a better, more mature individual," and "nothing in life is more important than having fun and being happy." The survey result means that even the most conservative Christian population is highly susceptible to the value system that comes through many channels in American society. The undermining goes on at a high rate even among the conservative evangelical Christians.

Having looked at the reality of the Christian retreat, we can now ask why it is happening. First, Christians are losing control of the institutions of our society. I am not able to give much attention to this here. But I do want to stress the fact that Christians are losing control of the opinion-forming institutions, especially the media and schools. A recent survey of media leaders shows that the media are predominantly in the hands of people who hold militantly un-Christian values; not just non-Christian values but un-Christian ones; not just holding them but holding them militantly.

Second, Christians are increasingly subject to the media, especially young Christians. The recent Search Institute survey I mentioned, about the good Christian children who turn out to be engaging so heavily in premarital sex, shows that these carly adolescent children spend an average of twenty-five hours a week looking at television, going to the movies, and that sort of thing. The most church-active among them manage only two hours a week in any sort of religious activity; a small minority of them spend as much as six hours a week in homework. Think of the proportion. What goes through their minds outside of school, hour after hour? Then we should add the factor of rock music, which many young people listen to as much as they possibly can. It is worth listening to the lyrics of popular music every so often to see how pernicious the messages are.

James Dobson makes the point when he says:

It's my conviction that the decay of traditional sexual morality, which we've seen in our society during the past decade particularly, is largely the result of avant-garde television programming and the movie industry. Each week producers seem determined to go a little further—to discuss the undiscussable and present the unpresentable. They assault the accepted standard of morality and decency night and day. It is also my opinion that this kind of trend in programming is not accidental. It is an intentional attempt to change the nation's mores and behavior, while earning a handsome profit in the process.

The third factor: there is less and less of a distinctively Christian social environment in which to grow up and live. The lack of a Christian environment is very important. We are affected by those around us. I just had an experience that I am sure would correspond to the experiences of many pastoral leaders. I noticed a person in our community suddenly expressing attitudes that I would consider non-Christian in a hedonistic direction. I tried to talk with him a bit to find out why this particular change was going on. I discovered that one of the chief things that had happened was that he had changed jobs and the new environment he was in—the management training course and the complex of attitudes among the people he worked with—was dominated by a hedonistic attitude.

Without thinking about it, he was picking up values and behavior patterns from the environment he was in. That, in fact, is the way it works for most of us unless we are particularly resistant to its happening. One can find a great deal of survey data that indicate how vulnerable we human beings are to the influence of the environment we live in. And so, if there are fewer and fewer Christian social environments, the attitudes, values, and behavior patterns of Christians are going to change for the worse. Here it is worth pointing out one of the results of the disintegration of Christian families. Whatever else one wants to say about the quality of Christian family life, fewer and fewer families are able to put together a strong home environment to counter what their young people are exposed to in society as a whole.

Finally, we can look at some underlying trends. We are not dealing with the propagandizing and political maneuvering of secularist forces. There are processes of change that are restructuring society in ways that make it very difficult to keep a distinctive way of life. The amount of time people spend using the media, for instance, is a social trend. One encounters the media all the time. To take another example, one of the factors that leads to the decline in church attendance is mobility. People move from one town to another and do not always connect with a church body. Mobility is on the rise, especially in the affluent, opinion-forming classes. A final example, just a small example of how daily life is reshaped by social trends so that it gets harder and harder to maintain the distinctive Christian way of life, came my way recently from a staff member of University Christian Outreach working at a state university in Maryland. He told me that in the dorms in his university there is not one corridor that is not mixed by sex. Quite often this also means bathrooms mixed by sex. In other words, one cannot live in the dorms in this new university without being among single men and women living in an absolutely unrestricted situation, with all kinds of sexual activity going on. One cannot get out of this situation if one is going to the university, other than by getting a room in town.

There are two reasons for pointing out the Christian retreat. First, we will not realize that we need to guard against the problem unless we know it is happening. I was talking not long ago with some Christians about why their youth group was not working well. They were saying that maybe they didn't do this right or that right, maybe another exciting new program would work, and so on. It was an interesting discussion, and they were identifying some good things. They probably could, in fact, make some improvements. But they neglected to observe that the social environment they were working in is a lot worse than it used to be, and so they should expect to find things harder. We do need to expect to have to do some things that we did not need to do ten years ago, much less twenty years ago. If we do not set that fact before us and realize that the environment is making it harder for us year by year, then we will not be in a good position to evaluate soberly how well we are dealing with a situation.

The second reason for pointing out the reality of Christian retreat is that it helps us see what it will cost to make a change. The worst part of it is, in fact, that it is going to cost more than we may want to pay. I was personally struck by hearing from William Ball about the *Wisconsin* v. *Yoder* case of several years ago in which Amish parents were prosecuted for not sending their children to high school. The Amish did not believe that "the higher learning," as they considered high school to be, was a helpful element in Christian living. Scripture uses the terminology of Christians being "on trial" in front of the world. The Amish had a great testimony to give. Whatever one thinks of their stand on education, one has to admit that their life together gives testimony to Christ. Their lawyer was able to bring it out by, for instance, asking the social workers and law enforcement officers called as witnesses whether any of the Amish young people wound up in jail for drunken driving or vandalism or whatever. The answer was no. Are they part of the drug-abuse problem? No. Are their people in the mental institutions? No. How many of them are in old-age institutions? None. Now there is a society that is functioning in a healthy way, taking none of the government budget for criminal protection and rehabilitation, family restoration, mental institutions, and so on. What one should want to find in a healthy, functioning society, the Amish have. God may one day say to the people who were in that courtroom, There you have the evidence of what Christianity can do in a group of people.

I would like to suggest that perhaps God might want to say something to us through the Amish. Are our churches and groups doing that well? If not, why do we not become more like the Amish? Now, to be clear, I think that there are some good answers. One reason why we do not want to be like the Amish is that the Amish do not do much evangelizing. To be sure, they evangelize more than people think they do, but their way of life as Amish does not seem to me to help in evangelism. Moreover, they do not have very much impact on society. At the same time, probably most of us do not even want to ask the question about whether we should consider doing something like what the Amish do. If we are going to be honest, there is a desire in us, that we do not want to acknowledge, to be a part of the world. We do not want to look strange. We do not want the media to have us up on stage, as it has some of the fundamentalist folks and the Amish every so often, and laugh at us. We do not want to be commented on adversely in the *Washington Post* or the *Ann Arbor News*. We want the world to accept us as respectable even though we have orthodox Christian beliefs. I believe all of us have that desire. I do. It is the worldly temptation. If we do not realize that we are grappling with it, we can be easily deceived.

I do not believe that we have to become like the Amish. But I do think that one key piece in the strategy that we have to evolve is a greater separation from the world. Most of us have to make bigger steps than we have been willing to make so far. For example, we cannot have all the sights and sounds of the secular mass media going through our minds and our children's minds, and expect to have a healthy, effective, distinctive way of life that is genuinely Christian. We have to learn to be decisive and firm about separation from the society around us in ways that break the influence of the non-Christian society on us.

On the other hand, there is something positive that we need to do as well as something negative. We need to build the kind of relationships with one another, the kind of day-in-and-day-out way of life, that become a real alternative to our secular society. This means we have to spend more time together than most surveys would indicate Christian people normally do. Our Christian sharing has got to reach into our daily lives. We can no longer rely just on the family. The family may have been strong enough twenty years ago, but it no longer is. We have to invest more in a whole way of life that forms an alternative to the secular way of life around us.

A rise in religious interest is not a rise in gospel living. We are deluded if we think it is. The Lord has called us to a new way of life and he wants us to live it. He is giving us the power and the wisdom to live it, but he also expects us to pay the price of Christian discipleship, to put the world behind us and the cross before us, and to live the full Christian way of life.

I want to conclude with a final comment on what we can learn from considering the Christian advance side as well. It is true some of us know the Christian retreat side only too well. We could use a little Gallup Poll Euphoria or faith-filled thinking, based on our faith in the power of God and the resurrection of Christ, to counter the discouragement we can feel because of the condition of things around us. There is a great responsiveness to and interest in the gospel. The decline of residual Christian values in American society leads to a greater sense of spiritual need. We want to take a look at our base of support, but we do not just want to shore ourselves up. We want to advance in the United States, and all the indications are that we can. Realism plus faith in Christ can lead to a true Christian optimism.

# Notes

1. Richard John Neuhaus, "Law and the Limits of Pluralism," *Christian Legal Society Quarterly,* Vol. 5, Number 1, 1984, p. 15.
2. Theodore Caplow, et al., *All Faithful People: Change and Continuity in Middletown's Religion* (Minneapolis: University of Minnesota, 1983), pp. 94-97.
3. Bryan Wilson, *Religion in Secular Society: A Sociological Comment,* 1966, p. 112.
4. *Young Adolescents and Their Parents* (Minneapolis: Search Institute, 1984), p. 3.
5. Paul M. Jacobson, *American Marriage and Divorce* (New York: Rinehart and Co., 1959), p. 90; Donald J. Bogue, *The Population of the United States* (New York: Free Press/Macmillan, 1985), p. 166.
6. Joseph E. Davis and Kevin Perrotta, "Finally, Figures on Divorce Among Christians," *Pastoral Renewal,* April 1984, pp. 120-122.
7. George Barna and William Paul McKay, *Vital Signs* (Westchester, Ill: Crossway Books, 1984), p. 11.
8. Joseph E. Davis and Kevin Perrotta, *op. cit.*
9. George Barna and William Paul McKay, *op. cit.*

# *Other Books of Interest*

### Christianity Confronts Modernity
*Edited by Peter Williamson and Kevin Perrotta*

Contains essays by Donald Bloesch, Stephen Clark, Paul Vitz, James Hitchcock, J.I. Packer, and others on the impact of modernity on Christian faith and morality. *$7.95*

### Summons to Faith and Renewal
*Edited by Peter Williamson and Kevin Perrotta*

J.I. Packer, Ralph Martin, Harold O.J. Brown, Stephen Clark, and others outline a strategy for Christian renewal in a post-Christian world. They urge Catholics, Protestants, and Orthodox to come together as brothers and sisters in Christ in order to deal with the new challenges that face the churches. *$7.95*

Available at your Christian bookstore or from
**Servant Publications • Dept. 209 • P.O. Box 7455
Ann Arbor, Michigan 48107**
Please include payment plus $.75 per book
for postage and handling
*Send for your FREE catalog of Christian
books, music, and cassettes.*